SUCCEED IN SPITE OF YOURSELF

SUCCEED IN SPITE OF YOURSELF

Everett T. Suters

VAN NOSTRAND REINHOLD COMPANY

New York   Cincinnati   Toronto   London   Melbourne

Van Nostrand Reinhold Company Regional Offices:
New York   Cincinnati   Chicago   Millbrae   Dallas

Van Nostrand Reinhold Company International Offices:
London   Toronto   Melbourne

Library of Congress Catalog Card Number: 73-7655
ISBN: 0-442-28077-7

Manufactured in the United States of America

Published by Van Nostrand Reinhold Company
450 West 33rd Street, New York, N.Y. 10001

Published simultaneously in Canada by
Van Nostrand Reinhold Ltd.

11   10   9   8   7   6   5   4   3   2   1

Library of Congress Cataloging in Publication Data

Suters, Everett Thomas.
    Succeed in spite of yourself.

    1. Success.   I. Title.
BJ1611.S884   1973   158'.1   73-7655
ISBN 0-442-28077-7

This book is dedicated to the two men
who have had the greatest influence
in enabling me to
SUCCEED IN SPITE OF MYSELF

———

Roger I. Hallock
Herbert E. Harris

Preface

No one can defeat us unless we first defeat ourselves.

—Dwight D. Eisenhower

The title of this book says it all. You *can Succeed in Spite of Yourself*. You are your own worst enemy, and how successful you will become is a function—not of how successful you are capable of being —but of how successful you are *willing* to be. We use only a fraction of our ability. We all have the capacity for becoming more successful than we already are.

This is a practical "How To Do It" (and "How *Not* To Do It") book about becoming successful. It is based on my business experiences over the last twenty-one years. This is not a hypothetical book or a digest of how others have become successful. In those instances where I have expressed a theory, it is only where I believe in the theory with deep conviction. The book is about my successes but it is also about my lack of successes (a euphemism for "making a hell of a lot of mistakes"). Throughout the book, I have liberally quoted others where they have well expressed my own strong feelings.

We often hear people say, "I wish that I had known then what I know now!" One of the objectives of this book is to give you the opportunity "to know now what I wish that I had known then." My "now" can be your "then." Why should you "reinvent the wheel?" The rest of us have reinvented it often enough. If you will open your mind, you can take advantage of my experience over the past twenty-one years in succeeding in spite of myself.

I am *fortunate* in having made many mistakes. The price of being wrong was cheap relative to the value of the lessons that I have learned. Hopefully, with this book, you will be able to take advantage of what I learned the hard way, without having to go through the same painful processes.

The last twenty-one years have given me an excellent laboratory experience in business. I was with Delta Air Lines for two years. I was a data processing salesman with IBM for four years, and then fifteen years as founder and President of Management Services, Inc., as well as being involved in other business interests. During this period, I have been an avid student of business success, theory and practice, some of which I have adopted as part of my own business philosophy.

Unfortunately, too many books on success have been written by unsuccessful writers who become successful by writing about how to be successful. I wrote this book, not for financial gain, but rather to summarize my business philosophy, and make it available to others. Ben Sweetland said, "We cannot hold a torch to light another's path without brightening our own." This project has enabled me to crystallize my own thinking; and I believe that I say some things of value in this book that will be of help to some of you who will invest your time in reading it.

Associating with others who are interested in success is a continuous learning process. We learn from each other. I would be in your debt if I might hear from any of you who would care to comment on the contents of this book or give me your thoughts relative to becoming successful.

Everett T. Suters

In helping others to succeed we insure our own success.
—*William Feather*

Contents

SUCCEED IN SPITE OF YOURSELF

What is Success?

To be what we are, and to become what we are capable of becoming, is the only end of life.

—Spinoza

I WAS TEMPTED not to write a chapter on "What is Success?" However, it would be inappropriate if I did not try to define success, at least as it applies to my experience. This is the first chapter of the book, but the last chapter to be written. I was in hopes that in the process of collecting my thoughts between these covers in the other chapters I would have been able to simplify my previous definition of success. This has not been the case.

Success is not simple. Neither is its definition. The attempt to define success can be more valuable than the definition itself. Perhaps, after you have read the rest of this book, you will reread the first chapter. You might find it more meaningful the second time around.

In order to define success, we must look for the characteristics of success. They are more important than the definition itself.

Success is "the satisfying of an individual's highest levels of need, above the biological level." Another way to express this same definition would be "the satisfying of an individual's *nonbiological* levels of need in the following *order*: security, being accepted by his fellow man, feeling important and experiencing a sense of self-fulfillment."

Why exclude the "biological level?" Because it is physical in nature, not mental. Success to a man lost in the desert may be a drink of water. Success to a seriously ill person may be the ability to continue breathing. It would be difficult to argue that this does not represent success. However, for the purposes of this book, we will concern ourselves with success as it pertains to a person's mental state.

Let's look at the characteristics of success.

1. *Personal.* Success is personal. Each of us must decide for himself what success is to *him*. I attended a seminar at which a speaker stated that success was *personal* and that it must be *worthwhile*. Based on this, the speaker indicated that Al Capone was not successful because what he did was not worthwhile. But this is open to question. I am not a member of the Al Capone or Adolph Hitler fan clubs, but if success is personal, how can I make the determination for them as to what was worthwhile? Capone and Hitler were not successful by *my* standards, but they might have been by *their own* standards. By my definition, being *worthwhile* is superfluous. If it is *personal*, I must decide if it is worthwhile.

2. *Mental.* Success is a state of the mind. If in *your mind* you are successful, then you are, in fact, successful. Success for an individual cannot be measured by financial or other tangible means unless it spells success in that person's mind. If you have ten million dollars, although you may be successful by someone else's standards, if you do not think yourself to be successful then you are not successful in spite of your millions.

3. *Relative.* No one is a complete success or a complete failure. You cannot say that Aristotle Onassis, Howard Hughes or John Paul Getty are complete successes, even by the standards of those preoccupied with money as a yardstick. If money is the measure, at what point was Onassis, Hughes or Getty successful? Was it one million? two million? fifty million?

You are the best "benchmark" of your own success. Other people give you perspective and guidelines, but the true measure of success on a relative basis is how well off you are now compared to what you were previously. A man who pulls himself up by his own bootstraps from nothing and ends up with $100,000 might be more successful financially, than another man who started off with one million dollars and twenty years later ends up with two million.

Financial yardsticks are easily understood. However, I feel that far too often we equate success with financial gain. If you feel that success does mean financial gain, consider Jesus Christ, Gandhi and Albert Schweitzer. Al Capone spilled more money on the way to the bank than these three gentlemen ever amassed all put together.

Two men died in a fall from the same bridge on the same night. One was a suicide who plunged to his death after having lost his millions and now had only $100,000 left. The other was a derelict who had won $100,000 in the Irish Sweepstakes. In his drunken stupor, celebrating his good fortune, he fell from the bridge accidentally. One man a failure, the other a success. Both with $100,000 as their measuring stick for success, or lack of success.

This would indicate that success is not only relative but it also has something to do with your direction—which brings us to the next characteristic.

4. *Progressive.* Success implies improvement or progress. In the example of the two men falling from the bridge,

each had the same amount of money, but they had gotten there from different directions. The key word is progress. The progressive nature of success has to be viewed over a long enough time span to be significant. It is difficult to look at success on a day-to-day basis. For example, although success is mental, if success to you represents how well you are doing in the stock market, you can not look at the day-to-day fluctuations with any degree of significance. If one day your stocks are up and the next day they are down, this does not make you successful one day and a failure the next. What you are interested in is how you are doing on a net basis over a given period of time. So it is with the progressive nature of success. Over a given period of time you need to know that you are making progress. A successful doctor may lose a patient occasionally, but this does not make the successful doctor a failure on the days that he loses more patients than he cures.

5. *Portable.* Inasmuch as success is personal and mental it is not a function of the job environment. However, the environment must provide a vehicle for success. You can have everything going for you and you may have a rough time trying to make it "big" with a tattoo shop. The elements of success have to be *within you*—not in the job environment itself.

Many of us have seen the show, *You Can't Take It With You.* If you are truly a successful person, you *Can* take it with you. Many people say that they were successful because of their particular job or career. While there are instances where this is true, most of the time this is not the case. Most people are not divinely inspired to do whatever it is that they are doing and they could be equally, if not more, successful in other pursuits. So take off the blinders to your environment. I have seen people leave a job, apparently after having been successful, and go into an entirely different field and become even more successful than they were before.

It is another case of succeeding in spite of yourself. You are giving credit for the success to the environment, when actually it was within you all of the time.

6. *Success has an appetite which grows at the higher levels of need.* Success is like a living organism that has to be fed. The higher your degree of success, the more you will require of yourself and the greater will be your appetite for more success. The appetite is more easily satisfied at the lower levels in the satisfying of the needs for security and being accepted by your fellow man. At the high levels of need involving the need to feel important and the need for experiencing a sense of self-fulfillment, these appetites are almost insatiable. As in the case of narcotics, it takes larger and larger doses to satisfy temporarily the need, but the appetite comes back stronger than ever.

7. *Transitory.* Success comes and goes. On balance you may feel successful most of the time, but at times you will obviously feel more successful than you do at others. When things are going your way it is easy to have a positive attitude and feel successful. It takes a strong mental discipline to maintain a positive attitude and a feeling of success when things are going against you. The transitory nature of success is understandable inasmuch as success is a state of the mind.

8. *Success can be vicarious.* You can experience success through the successes of others. Think of people working on the staffs of high government officials, and people working closely with the heads of business. Parents often experience success through their children. Wives experience a feeling of success through their husbands, secretaries through the people to whom they report, etc. In the case of wives particularly, they are often placed in a position where their best avenue to the feeling of success is to experience it through the success of their husbands.

I would suggest to women who are contemplating

marriage that they compare the need-level of a potential husband candidate with their own need-level of success. It is an unfortunate situation, to say the least, when the woman finds herself tied to the home with car pools and children and has a higher success-need than does her less ambitious husband. It makes for a very uncomfortable relationship. It is much better for the husband to have a higher level of success-need than does the wife.

9. *The attainment and nourishment of success can be largely mechanical.* This may sound like a contradiction. Success is *mental.* However, you can attain the mental attitude of success by mechanical or physical means. By the same means you can also further nourish the appetite for more success. In fact, the use of physical and mechanical means is a prerequisite for the mental state of success. (A large portion of this book has to do with the mechanical processes for achieving and maintaining success.)

10. *Success can be stunted, can wither and can fluctuate.* We may impose restrictions on our success—or they may be imposed on us by others. The restrictions that others impose upon us are usually more easily eliminated than the restrictions that we place on ourselves. We are able to be more objective about the restrictions that others place on us. They are obvious to us. We either take steps to eliminate these restrictions or we learn to live with them. We find ourselves in a job without any success potential and we can make a decision NOT to do anything about it. We decide to stay where we are and eventually our mental image of success begins to wither and we are willing to accept less and less.

Much more difficult is the stunting of success that we impose upon ourselves. The "world is our oyster" but we condition ourselves to become less than what we are capable of being. We are our own worst enemy, but by overcoming these self-imposed restrictions we can succeed in spite of ourselves.

The stunting or withering of our success does not have to be permanent. Where we have imposed the restrictions on ourselves we can reverse them *any time* that we decide that we want to reverse them.

Most of the restrictions that others impose upon us can be eliminated by recognizing these restrictions and taking appropriate steps to eliminate them. However, these restrictions are not always easy to eliminate. Gifted and ambitious people who found themselves in Nazi prison camps forgot their lofty ambitions in their quest to live. Our ideas of success can fluctuate, depending on the conditions.

11. *Success is NOT just a journey, but has "rest stops" and intermediate destinations that can become permanent destinations.* Many define success as a journey and not a destination. One of the major transportation companies used to have a slogan that "Getting there is half the fun." This is appropriate when referring to success. Getting there is some of the fun but it is not all of the fun. Reaching intermediate destinations is also a lot of the fun. People at times will "plateau out" for awhile before moving to higher levels. They enjoy the intermediate destination for a time and then they become bored with it and decide to go on to a higher level.

At one time I would have agreed that success is a journey and not a destination, but my observations and experience indicate that for some people success has been a journey and also a destination. Many people who appear to be successful and happy give no indication that they have any interest in continuing the journey.

12. *There is a sequence to success.* The process of becoming successful follows a logical sequence. However, this does not necessarily imply that you have to wait a long time before becoming successful. The sequence can be effected in a very limited time span, virtually overnight. You will become successful whenever you decide in your own mind that you are successful. The logical sequence of success is:

a. *Attitude.* "I want to be successful and I can be successful." Ernest Holmes wrote that "Life is a mirror and will reflect back to the thinker what he thinks into it."

Nothing can stop the man with the right mental attitude from achieving his goal; nothing on earth can help the man with the wrong mental attitude.

—W. W. Ziege

b. *Self-image.* "I can be greater than I am. I have untapped resources that will enable me to be successful. My success will depend on what is *in me,* not in the environment in which I find myself." Seneca said that "Most powerful is he who has himself in his own power."

The one and only formative power given to man is thought. By his thinking he not only makes character, but body and affairs, for "as he thinketh within himself, so is he."

—Charles Fillmore

c. *Perception.* With a positive attitude toward life and with a self-image that allows for greatness, we begin to see the world *positively*—and the world will see us accordingly. For every action there is a reaction. The world that counts is not so much the real world as is the one that you perceive. Daniel Webster said that "The world is governed more by appearances than by realities, so that it is fully as necessary to seem to know something as to know it."

Our life is what our thoughts make it. A man will find that as he alters his thoughts toward things and other people, things and other people will alter towards him.

—James Allen

d. *Need recognition.* With a positive attitude, a high regard for ourselves and a perception of life on a positive basis, we raise our sights to higher levels. We look beyond the lower need-levels of security and being accepted by our fellow man to that of a feeling of importance and experiencing a self-fulfillment, which is the ultimate goal of man.

e. *Motivation.* With needs established, we are motivated (moved to action) to satisfy these needs.

f. *Objectives.* We direct our action (motivation) toward those objectives which will satisfy our needs.

> You can do what you want to do, accomplish what you want to accomplish, attain any reasonable objective you may have in mind. . . . Not all of a sudden, perhaps, not in one swift and sweeping action of achievement . . . But you can do it gradually—day by day and play by play—if you want to do it, you will do it, if you work to do it, over a sufficiently long period of time.
>
> —William E. Holler

■ What About Happiness?

Happiness is not a characteristic of success. Happiness is a *result* of success. Success is the cause, happiness is the effect. Happiness is a by-product of a mental attitude of success. If happiness can be defined as a feeling or a state of well being, then I can say that when I am successful, I am happy. I can NOT be happy when I am NOT successful. In this sense, happiness and success are inseparable.

There you have it. This to me is what success is all about. My "own personal" success is to achieve objectives that satisfy my need for self-fulfillment, which is "to be able to fulfill myself as a creative, unique individual according to my own innate potentialities and within the limits of reality."

To decide what success means to you is a meaningful exercise. If you do not know where you are going, you cannot get lost and any road will take you there.

Some things have not changed since the dawn of history, and bid fair to last out time itself. One of these things is the capacity for greatness in man.

—Dr. William Clyde de Vane

■ No Man Is a Hero to His Valet (or *Himself*)

J. D. Batten in his book, *Beyond Management by Objectives* makes the following statement:

> Until you know what you have within yourself as an individual, you cannot know what you can give. All reasonably normal people are aware of themselves. They recognize approximately what their talents and worth are. . . .

Although I admire Mr. Batten very much and enjoyed *Beyond Management By Objectives*, as well as two other books of his which I recommend that you read: *Tough-Minded Management* and *Developing a Tough-Minded Climate For Results*, I disagree rather strongly with Mr. Batten. I am convinced it is an extremely rare person who knows what he has within himself, and who realizes approximately what his talents and worth are.

I once heard a man give a talk entitled "You Can Be Greater Than You Are." I would recoin that title to express my strong feeling that "You *Are Already* Greater Than YOU *Think* That You Are." We do what we have to do or what we want to do.

To say that you can be greater than you are implies an inner change. However, before we need to concern ourselves with being better than we are, we should first concern ourselves with *being as great as we already are.* Is it not logical to maximize our present capacity before attempting to expand what is already available at our disposal? Why worry about getting more inventory when you aren't using what you already have?

As to becoming greater than we are, of course you can become greater than you are. It is only natural for us to do so. Everyday is a learning process for most people. Our abilities and capacities are like muscles. The more we use them, the stronger they become. If we do not use our capacities and abilities they will—like muscles—weaken and perhaps disappear. However, whenever we decide that we want to reverse the atrophying process and restore our capabilities, as with a muscle, we can do so.

It is disturbing to read a book like *The Peter Principle* by Laurence Peter and Raymond Hull, which implies that a man is promoted to his level of incompetence, where he stays . . . that we finally reach the point where we have to run just as fast as we can just to stay even . . . that most of the work is therefore done by those who have not yet reached their level of incompetence.

This book is disturbing because it appears to discount the personal growth which most of us are capable of experiencing. I deny that there is a practical level of incompetence and that we have to run as fast as we can to stay even. There is no one who "runs as fast as he can." Everyone can run faster if he wants to do so.

In wartime, many men were able to accomplish great things when they were called on to do so, and many achieved what they did because they either *had to* or *wanted to*; and what they have accomplished since the end of the war has in no way approached what they were able to do during the war. This is another example of the fact that we can do what we want to do or have to do —even if it is more than we were willing to admit that we could do until called upon.

> You all have powers you never dreamed of. You can do things you never thought you could do. There are no limitations in what you can do except the limitations in your own mind as to what you cannot do. Don't think you cannot. Think you can.
>
> —Darwin P. Kingsley

The tragedy for many is the lesson that was lost. They had the golden opportunity to get a glimpse of their real untapped potential—only to fall back into their old patterns when they were no longer challenged. We look, but do not see. We hear, but do not listen. We are exposed to situations without learning.

Nevertheless, the lesson is there. We *are* greater than we *think* we are.

There is a saying that "No man is a hero to his valet." This should be expanded to read "No man is a hero to his valet, *or to himself, and even less so to himself*." Although the valet sees the unimportant and is blinded by it to the extent that he cannot see many of the outstanding characteristics of the man he serves, we are even more blind toward ourselves. The valet can not see our self-doubts when we are acting confident and self-assured. He cannot see the "butterflies" in our stomachs when we are cool and collected on the outside. He cannot see the internal effects of frustration, disappointment, deep concern and worry. In many respects, we are like a Hollywood set with a main street made up of buildings with just "fronts." We show that which we want to be seen. The facade covers up much that cannot be seen except by ourselves.

We have self-doubts. We look at our fellow man and—although he also has self-doubts—he appears not to have them, which tends to make our situation even worse. What we do not realize is that we are affecting him the same way. We are like actors on a stage, acting the part of the person that we want to be, while our fellow man is doing the same thing.

You may have seen a television program called "To Tell The Truth." On this program, three contestants all claim to be a certain person. The panel must decide by asking questions which of the three people is telling the truth. It is amazing how often the panel is wrong in identifying the right person. This is the way that we are in life. Some people act more like they really are than others. When the difference between what a person is and what he acts like he is, is too great, we intuitively get a feeling that this person is a "phony," without knowing exactly why we feel that way. This television show is living proof to me of how we fool each other as to what we really are.

If we can replace a large part of this facade with a better recognition of our capabilities and talents, we begin to present an image to the world that is more like our true self, which in turn builds up our credibility in dealing with others. The more slight the difference between the person we project and the person we really are, the greater our credibility, our ability to communicate with others and our acceptance for what we are.

We are our own worst enemy, but we can succeed in spite of ourselves if we will just decide to quit preconditioning ourselves to accepting mediocrity and failure and quit looking for reasons why we *cannot* do something and instead view ourselves in a positive mode and ask ourselves "What do we have to do to accomplish that which we want to do?"

The space program stands out as the all time great monument to man's ability to do that which he decides he wants to do. The question was not "Why can't we go to the moon?" The question was "What are we going to have to do to get to the moon?" What a lesson this can be for all of us whenever we are confronted with what appears to be overwhelming obstacles. Do we say, "I can't do it because. . . ." or do we say, "I can do it by doing the following. . . ."?

> Within us all there are wells of thought and dynamos of energy which are not suspected until emergencies arise. Then oftentimes we find that it is comparatively simple to double or treble our former capacities and to amaze ourselves by the results achieved.
>
> —Thomas J. Watson

■ Above the Timberline

> In spite of the fact that the ladder tapers to one-man rungs at the top, the roomiest part is farthest up.
>
> —Charles R. Gow

As a concrete example of how you can "succeed in spite of yourself" and how you can raise yourself "above the timber line," I would like to relate to you how I happened to write this book.

When I first started thinking about the possibility of writing a book, I had a tendency to dismiss the idea for several reasons. I had never taken a writing course in school or had any experience in the field of journalism. I had no reason to believe that I had any particular aptitude for writing as I had never previously done any writing. Then I thought about the thousands of people who make a living by writing. I thought about the fact that I am not well-known as an author or otherwise, and then I read an article that indicated that on the average only one book out of every one hundred books that are submitted by unknown writers to publishers ever gets published and that only one book out of every ten submitted by known writers is published.

At this point it would have been very easy for me to abandon the idea of writing a book, except *for one important thing*. I do have a deep conviction, as the title of this book suggests, that YOU CAN SUCCEED IN SPITE OF YOURSELF. I was my own worst enemy. If I could eliminate some of my "hang-ups" or excuses for NOT writing a book, that would only leave me with the reasons why I *could* successfully write a book. I approached the situation on the basis of the reasons why I *should* write this book. What did I have to lose? What were the negatives that I had to contend with? Considering the negatives is not being pessimistic or having a negative attitude; it is an integral part of a realistic approach to any situation. You should always consider the negatives—make a risk assessment. But you should approach the negative aspects of any situation on a positive basis, asking yourself, "How am I going to be able to overcome the negatives in order to achieve that which I have decided that I want to achieve?"

Therefore, I approached the negative considerations as follows: As to not having any journalistic training with an unknown degree of aptitude, I asked myself which was more important, my journalistic style or what I have to say? The answer was obvious.

As to not being a professional writer, I decided that unless I wanted to write a book on being a professional writer it would not be a handicap. My topic was success. It seemed to me that being successful was a far more important qualification than training in writing.

From the standpoint of the difficulty of having a book published by an unknown writer, I figured that my chances were *at least* as good as any other unknown writer, which I considered to be pretty good odds.

In reviewing the negatives, it also became obvious to me that they were mostly mechanical in nature and had very little to do with the intrinsic value of anything that I had to say.

There is an old expression that "you should not throw the baby out with the bathwater." Don't throw the positive things out with the negative things. The idea is to throw out the negative leaving the positive. When I was a kid there was a popular song that I used to like, by Johnny Mercer, entitled "Accentuate the Positive." The song gave the very sound advice that you have to accentuate the positive and eliminate the negative. That's what it is all about, deceptively simple, yet very fundamental.

Having eliminated the negatives, I started looking for all of the reasons why I *could* write a book of value, that would be published.

For openers, I could literally eliminate as potential competition millions of people who have no interest in writing a book and will never write a book, for whatever their reasons. Out of the relatively few people left who will write books, many of them are professional writers who have not had the opportunity to experience what I have experienced and could, therefore, not write with the same degree of insight. I then eliminated all of the nonprofessional writers who have no interest in writing a book on being successful.

Finally, I came down to a very small group of businessmen, who have achieved some degree of success, who have the desire and will expend the effort necessary to write a book. When I looked at this very small group, I could not think of any reason why I should not write this book.

I have gone through this process many times in many different situations. It has worked on many occasions, but it doesn't always. It has worked enough times, however, that "you can't knock it if you haven't tried it."

In climbing a mountain, as you get to the higher elevations, the trees begin to thin out. The higher you go, the fewer the trees until finally you get to a point that is referred to as being "above the timber line" where trees do not grow. The trees are a lot like people moving up in their respective groups. As you begin to move up, you find that more and more people begin to plateau out and finally you get up near the timber line and there is not much competition. As you look back at all of the people who are far behind you, you realize that you got there not because you went faster, necessarily, but because you just kept going. That is what success is all about. It is often a trip, not a destination. With success you keep moving to higher and higher levels, always setting goals, achieving them, and setting new goals. Those who have stopped somewhere along the way can start up again any time they want to.

You may say that your idea of success "is being able to sit on your rear-end and do nothing." But the alternative to success is not necessarily failure, but rather a "lack of success," which puts you in a category of a "failure-avoider." Wanting to get to the point that you do not have to do anything is a very hollow goal.

The irony of this situation is that the characteristics which you have that will enable you to become successful are usually the very characteristics that will not allow you to quit achieving more and more success. It becomes your *nature* to want to achieve, you can not turn it off like a water faucet. To stop achieving and growing for a "success-seeker" is to become a psychological vegetable.

Let's consider what "leisure" means. Once, at a trade association meeting, I had lunch with a gentleman who had spoken that morning on the more effective use of time. During lunch he asked me how many hours a week I normally devoted to business activities. When I told him that I put in about sixty hours per week, he immediately replied that I was doing something wrong and that I should be able to get my "work" done in forty hours per week. I then asked him what the hell I was supposed to do with the twenty hours that I would no longer be devoting to my business activities. He suggested that I take up golf. (At this point I was about to suggest what he could do.) I indicated that I used to play golf but enjoyed business much more; so I quit playing golf and devoted more time to business. Now I had this gentleman on the ropes; so, I moved in for the "kill." I told him that although I felt that I was already well-organized and used my time effectively, I would love to be able to be more efficient. Not that I would put in any fewer hours. I would just like to be able to get more done in the same number of hours that I now devote to business.

I am not obsessed with business, and I recognize the importance of keeping balance in your life. I spend plenty of time with my family. I go fishing about one day per week for nine months out of the year, and I have many other interests outside of business. One advantage that I probably have over most people is that I require very little sleep. I normally go to bed at 2:15 A.M. and get up at 7:30 A.M. This in itself gives me the equivalent of approximately eighteen more waking hours per week than the average person. I do not feel that I am overworked.

Most people who are making something happen are not overworked. The "overworked executive" is a myth. People only appear to be overworked because they get so absorbed in what they are doing. Most of them are putting in the hours that they do because they want to, not because they have to. At the end of each week they have accomplished more, derived more satisfaction from their jobs, and are less physically tired than their forty-hour per week, clockwatching counterparts.

Speaking of forty-hour weeks, it is not my intention to be critical of unions, and I recognize the great amount of good they have done, but I do think it is unfortunate that they have brought pressure to bear for shorter work weeks instead of putting more emphasis on job satisfaction and enrichment and a deep sense of involvement in the job itself. There is no way that success-seeking people will begin to work a shorter work week, the unions notwithstanding. In the case of management, they will continue to put in pretty much the same number of hours. If this is so and union members further shorten their work week, industry will have to follow suit and shorten the work week for all of their nonmanagement people. The unfortunate result will be that a large segment of the population will be further discouraged from achieving success in their jobs. Many who are success-seekers will "moonlight" and will hold down two jobs, each of almost equal duration, thus cutting down on the time put in on one job. The fragmenting of their efforts into two jobs will compound the problem of low job satisfaction.

> I am glad that the eight-hour day had not been invented when I was a young man. If my life had been made up of eight-hour days I do not believe I could have accomplished a great deal. This country would not amount to as much as it does if the young men of fifty years ago had been afraid that they might earn more than they were paid for.
> —Thomas A. Edison

Motivating Yourself and Others

People may change their minds as often as their coats, and new sets of rules of conduct may be written every week, but the fact remains that human nature has not changed and does not change, that inherent human beliefs stay the same; the fundamental rules of human conduct continue to hold.

—Lammot du Pont

MOTIVATION is a thread that runs through the fabric of everything else that is in this book. Motivation is the fuel that will make success happen. Nothing in the book is of value without the element of motivation.

Motivation "is action directed toward objectives for the purpose of satisfying needs."

Every action that we take is the result of some kind of stimulus or motivation. When you are sufficiently motivated, *you will succeed in spite of yourself.*

If you cannot become motivated to want to succeed, you will

not succeed no matter how much knowledge and expertise you may have. You can possess all of the good qualities and you may know HOW you can succeed, but motivation is the necessary power supply.

When we understand what motivates us, we can offset many of our deficiencies. If you can create a climate in which people will motivate themselves to do that which you want them to do, there is no limit to the amount of success you can expect to achieve.

You cannot "motivate people." Most psychologists and students of motivation believe that you can only create a situation or a climate in which people will motivate themselves. The difference is significant. I can "move" an individual. I can "make" him do something if I apply enough pressure or if I am able to manipulate or "trick" him. I can drive "bamboo shoots" under your fingernails and you will probably do what I want you to do, but this is not motivation. This is movement. Veterans of the armed forces know that the sergeants and chief petty officers used movement, not motivation.

There are basically three ways that people are moved to action:

1. Intimidation
2. Manipulation
3. Motivation

When you intimidate people, they move through fear of punishment, and as long as you are around or can exercise ironclad control, they will act in the manner in which you want them to act, but they will not be doing as much as they are capable of doing. They will do only enough to satisfy the intimidator and to escape the fear of punishment. The galley slaves in the middle ages rowed just hard enough to keep the whip off their backs. The objective was to conserve energy and attempt to survive. You can bet that they spent very little time thinking about becoming more productive or seeking success.

People are also moved to action by being manipulated. Manipulation is more effective than intimidation *for a short period of time*—because people *think* they are doing things because they want to do them. However, there comes the inevitable moment of truth when those who are being manipulated realize that they have been "had"; "conned"; taken advantage of. After this moment of truth, manipulation is almost totally ineffective. It leaves most people with the attitude that: "Fool me once, shame on you. Fool me twice, shame on me."

At least intimidation is honest. When you are being intimidated by someone, he makes no pretense of doing anything else. General Patton was well known for intimidating people (and was quite successful at it). However, things are a little different in the military. If people quit, you can always have them shot! Patton was honest about it. His people knew that they were being intimidated.

Motivation is the third—and by far the best—way to lead people to act. When you move people, you do it *to* them. When they are motivated, it comes from *within*. People can achieve that which they are *motivated to achieve*. They can overcome problems, difficulties, deficiencies in their make-up. In short, when they are motivated, *they will succeed in spite of themselves*.

The great value in the study and observation of what motivates people is that in the process of learning what motivates other people, you learn what motivates you. Socrates said, "Know Thyself." It is logical to assume that you can *motivate yourself* more effectively if you are aware of *what* motivates you.

A basic understanding of the theory of motivation is extremely valuable, if not essential, in finding out what motivates you. Motivation theory precedes the practice of motivation; and the two are inseparable.

You may already be highly motivated—without ever hearing of motivation theory. You may feel that you do not need to know why *you* are motivated as long as you *are* highly motivated. But it is still vital to understand what motivates *other* people. When you begin to understand what will make people act in a predetermined way, then, brother, you are on your way to success.

Consider the demanding job of selling. THE most important asset a good salesman can have is an understanding of what will motivate his prospect to action. We are all salesmen in the sense that we will succeed largely by our ability to create situations in which other people will take action in a way that we have predetermined.

Let's take a look at motivation theory. I am a great admirer and disciple of Abraham Maslow and Frederick Herzberg. Both of these gentlemen have had a profound effect on my thinking for which I am in their debt. I hope that I will be able to encourage many of you to read the works of these men for more information on this fascinating subject.

Abraham Maslow takes the position that people are motivated because of what they perceive in their minds as a need. Whether the need is real or imagined is not so important as what they "think" they need. So if need is what causes people to be motivated, we should first analyze needs. Maslow developed what he called a Hierarchy of Needs in which he established a ranking of five levels of need. From lowest to highest, the levels of man's needs are: (1) *biological* or *animal*; (2) *security*; (3) *social* or *group acceptance*; (4) *ego* or *feeling of importance*; (5) *self-fulfillment* We first satisfy the lower level needs, then progress to the highest level of need as each successive level is satisfied. Let's examine each level.

Biological needs. These are needs with which we are all born. They include the need for food, water, warmth, fresh air, etc. These are basic animal needs, and in this respect man is very little different from an animal.

Security needs. After man has satisfied his biological needs, he then looks to security or safety, (*but only* after he has satisfied his biological needs). When I was a kid I used to go to the cowboy movies on Saturday and watch the cowboys sneak past the Indians to the water hole for a drink of water. Their drive for the biological need for water was stronger than their need for safety or security.

Social or group acceptance. At this point man has plenty to eat and drink and is warm and secure. He now begins to want to be accepted by the group. He wants to be a part of society.

Ego or feeling of importance. Now that man is fat, secure and "one of the boys," he wants to be more than just "one of the boys." He craves recognition, he wants to feel important. He might be the Indian who carves the totem pole out of a tree at the entrance to the Indian camp, or the executive who wants the key to the executive washroom.

Self-fulfillment. This is the highest need-level of man—to get a sense of fulfillment, the realization that he is utilizing his capabilities to the fullest. At this point, he is more interested in how he judges himself than how he is judged by others. As opposed to the Indian who carved a totem pole at the entrance to the camp for his ego, this Indian might have carved a totem pole in the deepest part of the forest; an accomplishment that only he knew about. This is the executive who moves about virtually unnoticed making things happen with very little regard to who else knows it, as long as *he* knows it. These are the Howard Hughes types who once basked in the limelight, but having moved through the *ego* level no longer *need* ego gratification or a feeling of importance.

A fascinating gentleman by the name of Frederick Herzberg came along and used Maslow's Hierarchy Of Needs to develop what he called a "Motivation-Hygiene Theory." Perhaps the easiest way to get a basic understanding of the theory is to follow this simple diagram:

NEED

5. Self-fulfillment				
4. Ego or feeling of importance	Motivators →	Work Itself	→ Job Enrichment	→ Happy

· ·

3. Social or group acceptance				
2. Security or safety	Satisfiers or → Hygiene	Things in the Work	→ No Job Enrichment	→ Unhappy
1. Biological or animal	Factors	Environment		

Herzberg's theory is that the needs above the dotted line (ego and self-fulfillment) are the things which motivate people, and that when people are motivated, they are happy. He also takes the position that the things that motivate people have to do with the work itself and not the things that exist in the job environment (like benefits, fancy office, retirement plans, etc.)

Herzberg then says that the needs below the dotted line (biological or animal, security or safety, and social or group acceptance) are needs that can only be satisfied, but will *not* result in a person being motivated. These needs are hygienic in nature. The satisfying of hygienic needs only serves to "keep the atmosphere clean." He uses the example of garbage disposal. Garbage disposal is hygienic in nature in that it does not make you healthy, but keeps you from being *un*healthy. By satisfying the lower level of needs we can only hope to keep ourselves or other people from being unhappy. Therefore, the things that make you unhappy are not the opposite of those things which make you happy. Satisfying the lower level of needs brings you back to zero, but does not make you happy or motivate you.

Herzberg has also done a great deal of work in the area of job enrichment. You can enrich jobs through the satisfaction of those needs above the line (ego and self-fulfillment), but you cannot enrich a job with the satisfaction of the lower level of needs below the line. Herzberg makes the point that if you cannot enrich a job, it had better have plenty of hygiene (or satisfiers) to make up for the lack of enrichment. Lack of job enrichment can result in morale problems. There will always be dull, insipid jobs that cannot be enriched. Many of these will eventually be automated out. Our challenge is to identify our own need-level and the need-levels of those who report to us and attempt to match the need-level of the individual with the requirements of the job to be done. If you have a job requiring someone to shovel horse manure all day long, you had better try to find an individual whose need-level (probably biological or animal) is such that he is content to shovel manure. (No offense intended to you manure shovelers.)

Motivation theory is not a science. It is an art that has to be practiced. You cannot permanently "peg" people at any given need-level. Our need-levels fluctuate up and down, and we are all motivated by the different levels of need to some degree. It has been said that an ambitious man lost in the desert forgets his ambitions in quest for water. Job-seekers who are out of work will often take on the characteristics of someone trying to satisfy the lower levels of need and will appear not to be success-seekers. It is necessary to look beyond this impression, because a man out of work obviously IS temporarily concerned with satisfying his lower level of need and should be evaluated accordingly.

Up to this point, we have not considered money as a need or a motivator—for good reason. *Money is not a need and it is not a motivator.* This requires some explaining. There are behavioral scientists who go around the country on speaking engagements giving people the impression that they do not think that money is important. Yet these behavioral scientists will not come and speak to you for less than five hundred to one thousand bucks per engagement.

Money *is important*—but no one *needs* money. Money is only a satisfier of a need. I may be hungry (biological), deep in debt (need for security) and want to live in a better neighborhood (social or group acceptance). Money can satisfy these lower level needs by getting me something to eat, getting me out of debt and enabling me to move to a better neighborhood. Money is a SATISFIER of a need, it is *not a need.*

At the higher levels of need, you do not require money in itself. You need ego and self-fulfillment. Money can satisfy these needs if you can go out and buy a Rolls Royce and satisfy your ego need, and donate a million dollars anonymously to your old alma mater to satisfy your need for self-fulfillment. But you do not necessarily have to spend money to satisfy the needs for ego and self-fulfillment.

I am NOT knocking the fact that people want money, but before I can understand what motivates a person I have to find out what it is that he wants the money for. If I am trying to hire a new salesman, I had much rather he would tell me that he wants to make money than to tell me that he wants to serve his fellow man. He may get the "Mr. Nice Guy" award out in the territory, but in the meantime he is probably giving away the store. If you can get a person to tell you why he wants to make money, he will be telling you the need that he wants to satisfy and therefore what motivates him. If a man wants to make money because he is hungry and wants something to eat, how are you going to create a situation in which he will remain motivated after he is eating regularly? If he tells you that he wants to save enough money to buy the Empire State Building, you can hang a big picture of the building in front of his desk and know that he will be "turned on" for awhile.

The secret is to *create an environment* in which people will be motivated to satisfy their need for ego and self-fulfillment. Unlike the appetites for food, security, and group acceptance, the appetites for ego and self-fulfillment are very difficult to satisfy. The more you get, the more you want, which results in a high degree of motivation.

I defined motivation as, "action directed toward objectives for the purpose of satisfying needs." The sequence is therefore established of *need* which results in *motivation* toward an *objective*.

> The very essence of all power to influence lies in getting the other person to participate. The mind that can do that has a powerful leverage on his human world.
> —Harry A. Overstreet

■ The Chicken or the Egg (Front-end Effort)

> No student ever attains very eminent success by simply doing what is required of him; it is the amount and excellence of what is over and above the required, that determines the greatest of ultimate distinction.
> —Charles Kendall Adams

All of our lives we have heard the question, Which came first, the chicken or the egg? I think of this when the question is posed: "Do you first put in the effort and then expect to get compensated for it, or do you expect to be assured of the compensation before you are willing to put in the effort?" The answer is obvious, and if I were to be able to choose the one thing in this book that I would most desire to impress upon the reader it would be that, IF YOU WILL DO MORE WORK THAN YOU ARE PAID FOR, YOU WILL ULTIMATELY BE PAID FOR MORE WORK THAN YOU DO. I heard this years ago when I first went into my own business, and was putting in eighty and one hundred hours per week and making far less money than I did while I was with IBM.

We can chart the principle like this:

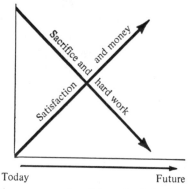

There are several reasons why this principle is sound and logical. The first consideration is that putting in "FRONT END EFFORT" is very much like putting money in a savings account and then taking advantage of the compounded interest. Let's assume that over a ten-year period you save one thousand dollars and put it into a savings account. You obviously will end up with a much greater return after ten years if you had saved the bulk of the thousand dollars in the early years and let it work for you in the later years than would be the case if you saved very little money in the early days and saved the bulk of the money toward the end of the ten-year period. Putting the money in toward the end of the period would leave very little time for your money to work for you.

So it is with front end effort. By giving your job your very best efforts and learning all that you can as early in the game as possible, you put "money in the bank" that begins to work and compound for you. If you do this early enough you will be able to:

1. Test your organization.
2. Build up momentum and move ahead of the pack.
3. Acquire knowledge, experience and a greater interest in your work.
4. Get the attention of those around you.
5. Be insured against becoming "overage in rank."
6. Become goal-oriented.
7. Get back in return much more than you put in.
8. Capitalize on the slight edge.

Front end effort is important not just to young people beginning their careers. This principle is good for anyone regardless of his age and position. Starting tomorrow morning you can begin to build an edge over where you would be without following this principle. There are hundreds, if not thousands, of instances of people becoming successful late in their careers. Unlike a professional football player who has a limited number of years in which he can play the game, a business player *can make up his mind* to start playing well at any age and should continue to get better as time goes on.

Thomas J. Watson was forty years old when he founded what was to be the IBM Corporation. In spite of the fact that at forty he was almost broke and out of a job, he became one of the greatest business leaders of his time. John Patterson, who founded the National Cash Register Company, had enjoyed an unspectacular career as a coal dealer until he was past forty years of age. Colonel Sanders of Kentucky Fried Chicken fame was broke and living out of his car when he was in his sixties. Conrad Hilton was middle-aged before he realized the fruits of his early struggles. Arthur Vinings Davis retired as Chairman of Alcoa and went to Florida in his eighties to start another very successful career in the real estate business. It is never too late.

No age or time of life, no position or circumstance, has a monopoly on success. Any age is the right age to start doing!
—Gerard

When you do more than what you are paid for, the burden of making up for the deficit is shifted from you to your organization. When you do less or just as much as you are paid for, the organization rightfully has no particular incentive to give you more money, responsibility, etc. You are on the defensive, for the organization is really carrying you. Other people are making up for your deficit. You really put the organization to the test when you do *more* than you are paid for. Now you can properly assess—perhaps for the first time—if you are with the "right" organization. Is it an organization that recognizes outstanding performance and compensates you accordingly? You may either insist that you be put into a position in the company where you can progress, or you may decide to get out.

With front end effort you build up momentum and begin to move ahead of the pack. You will find that most of your fellow men are not really going anywhere. They are adrift. They are content to show just enough initiative to get by. And, when you begin to move ahead of the pack, you will find that it is much less crowded. In watching the Indianapolis 500 race, I have often thought that the race cars were a lot like men. The ones that move ahead of the pack have smooth sailing with very little traffic ahead of them; the cars behind them are all jammed-up together, eating the dust from those in front of the pack. You should not burn yourself out early in the race; however, expending that extra effort to get ahead of the pack will enable you to move ahead faster with less effort.

You will acquire more knowledge of what you are doing as well as more experience. As you develop expertise, you naturally will become more interested in what you are doing, with the result that you will do a much better job. How well you do almost anything is a result of the degree of interest that you have in it. As you do better, you get more interested. As you get more interested, you do better. It is a never-ending beneficial cycle that feeds on itself.

However, if you develop a dislike for what you are doing, the cycle can run in reverse. You do poorly; you get less interested. As you get less interested, you do even more poorly, and so on down. Someone once wisely said that the last day that you will ever really "work", is the day that you fall in love with what you are doing.

Obviously, as you begin to move ahead of the pack, you will begin to get the attention of those around you. Not only will the pack see you move out, but the others who are ahead of the pack will also notice you. The Good Book tells us that we should not "hide our light under a bushel." You will become your own best public relations agent when you expend the extra effort. People who are "turned on" are a very scarce commodity in any organization, and you will find that the people to whom you answer will begin concentrating on how they can best utilize your talents. You will eliminate the danger of being pigeonholed and getting lost in the shuffle.

Putting in the extra effort is the best insurance against becoming "overage in rank," to borrow an expression from the army. In the army, if you have not reached a certain rank as an officer by the time you are a certain age, they classify you as being "overage in rank." Business is not quite as rigid, but the danger is still there. There are many companies that will not hire or promote a person over a certain age. They feel that he does not have enough time left with the company to be of benefit to the organization in that capacity. Even if you are "overage in rank" right now, by putting in the extra effort you should be able to greatly enhance your chances of moving ahead; but even without being able to progress much further, you can still have the other benefits of beginning to do more than what you are paid to do. To be perfectly candid, it might mean the difference between keeping your job and losing it.

When you concentrate on doing more than you are paid for, it shifts your attention from the details of your job to goals—of your organization and your personal goals. When you do less than you are supposed to do, you become task-oriented. Your job gets all the attention because you are not really keeping up with its requirements. You don't control the job; the job controls you. When you do more than you are paid for, you have your job under control, and you have surplus capacity to be expended toward the goals of the company and making certain that your goals are compatible with those of your organization.

Front end effort will give you back in return much more than you put into your work. Many students never study until it is time for exams. Then they stay up all night "cramming." Not only do they get poor grades, but a week after the course is over they usually have no idea of what the course was all about. If they had put in the front end effort and had studied as hard during the first week of the course as during the last week, the same investment in time would have returned much greater dividends because of the momentum created at the beginning. Take the example of a salesman making prospect calls during the year. He will do much better for the whole year if he expends extra effort during the first part of the year in making a lot of calls, getting a lot of "irons in the fire" and stirring up interest in general. He will find that this early momentum will begin to reap a harvest as the year goes on. If he "goofs off" all year and then suddenly turns on the steam the last two months, he will probably do much worse for the year than the man who turned on the steam for the first two months of the year.

You will capitalize on the slight edge. You will find as you begin to move ahead of the pack that you will begin to be compensated, disproportionately perhaps, for the slight edge that you now have over what you previously had. The reason for this is that as the competition begins to thin out ahead of the pack, there are fewer people around who are accomplishing what you can do. This, for example, is why a baseball player batting .250 may get paid $25,000 per year, and a player batting .300 might make $75,000 per year. He gets two hundred per cent more compensation for twenty per cent better performance.

Some feel that "the game is not worth the candle," that the success you will achieve is not worth the sacrifice of putting in the extra effort on the front end. They are wrong. You either make a small sacrifice now, on the front end, or you make a much bigger sacrifice later. A year of extra effort now might very well result in high pay and great job satisfaction for the rest of your business careeer, as opposed to not putting in the extra effort now and being confined to the "pack" for the rest of your business career with average pay and without a sense of self-fulfillment. Look around you. The guys you see driving around in the big cars and spending the winters in Florida are the ones, for the most part, that at some point decided to do more than what they were paid to do. The others are still "grubbing it out," doing no more or no less than they have always done just waiting for their social security to take effect.

Henry Ford must have had pretty much the same philosophy when he said:

The man who will use his skill and constructive imagination to see how much he can give for a dollar, instead of how little he can give for a dollar, is bound to succeed.

(Henry Ford ought to know!)

■ Don't Catch the Mechanical Rabbit

Nothing is really work unless you would rather be doing something else.
—Chub De Wolfe

Have you ever seen a dog race? Perhaps the most fascinating thing about it is the mechanical rabbit that is kept just out of the reach of the racing dogs. The dogs really don't want to *catch* the rabbit. What they want to do is CHASE the rabbit. If by chance a dog ever overtook the rabbit, he would be disappointed by the hollow victory.

Doesn't this apply to the pursuit of success? The success is in the pursuit, not in the attainment. Success is as much a journey as a destination.

Several years ago Budd Schulberg wrote a book entitled *What Makes Sammy Run?*. The book was about Sammy Glick, who had tremendous drive and was obsessed with the achievement of more and more success and power. The question that was asked by many of the characters in the book was, "What makes Sammy run?" Why does he continue to pursue more and more success long after he seems to have attained all that he would possibly need? I believe that the people who would ask such a question probably would have a hard time understanding the answer even if it were given to them. They probably would not understand that the answer was simply—Sammy liked to run.

I know a man who spent eighteen years building a business by working night and day, almost every day of the week, taking infrequent vacations. While he was still in his forties, he sold his business to a large national company and retired. He said that he had worked hard for years and now he was going to really take it easy and enjoy himself. He had plenty of money and didn't *need* to work any more. Two months later he was fully involved in the real estate business, buying land, putting up office buildings, etc. This should come as no surprise. Once you have been in the parade, it is very hard to stay out of it.

Another example comes from *The Money Game* by Adam Smith:

> They came to the market to make money, and they told themselves that what they wanted was the money: security, a trip around the world, a new sloop, a country estate, an art collection, a Caribbean house for cold winters. And they succeeded. So they sat on the dock of the Caribbean home, chatting with their art dealers and gazing fondly at the new sloop, and after awhile it was a bit flat. Something was missing. If you are a successful Game player, it can be a fascinating, consuming, totally absorbing experience, in fact it has to be. If it is not totally absorbing you are not likely to be among the most successful, because you are competing with those who do find it so absorbing.
>
> The lads with the Caribbean houses and the new sloops, did not, upon the discovery that something was missing, sell those trophies and acquire sackcloth and ashes. The sloops and the houses and the art are still there, but the players have gone back to the Game, and they don't have a great deal of time for their toys. The Game is more fun . . . money is the way we keep score. But the real object of the Game is not money, it is the playing of the Game itself. For the true players, you could take all the trophies away and substitute plastic beads or whale's teeth; as long as there is a way to keep score, they will play.

To these people, money was like the mechanical rabbit. They thought money was what they wanted, but when they caught it they discovered that what they really wanted was to play the "Game." The tragic thing about so many people is that they spend their lives and careers pursuing what they *think* they want to the exclusion of everything else, often with a high degree of frustration. Then they discover too late that their success would have been in the journey, not in the destination. They discover only too late that money is a symbol and represents a *means* to an end, but is not an *end* in itself.

Another fundamental in the passage from *The Money Game* is that if you want to succeed you have to learn to love the game. If you don't, you are not likely to succeed because what is work to you is fun to someone else doing the same thing. For example, I do not care for playing golf. Let's assume that you love golf, and you and I went out this afternoon and played eighteen holes together. Even though I might have more native ability to play golf than do you, because of the fact that you love to play the game and I don't, it is highly unlikely that I would be able to compete effectively with you. So it is in business or in the pursuit of any career. The conclusion is simple. Learn to love what you are now doing; find something else to do that you can learn to love; or face the unpleasant alternative of spending the rest of your working life being miserable with limited chances for success. If you have to work, you might as well love it, and the last day that you will ever really *work*, is the day before you fall in love with what you are doing. From that day on, it will not be work, it will be fun.

The next lesson we can learn is that many people are fortunate enough to achieve what they THINK they want early enough in the game to realize that what they really liked was the Game. They have gained perspective and now they leave their trophies and symbols of success and go back to the Game because it is more fun. And when they go back, they are better players with the realization that what they love really is the Game.

The last lesson is that as they go back to the game with the realization that they love to play, it becomes obvious to them that money was the way of *keeping score* and for this reason is very important. They would still play even if it were not for money, IF THEY HAD A WAY TO KEEP SCORE. The score is very important because it provides a measurement. If two golfers of equal ability went out for a round of golf together and one golfer counted the number of strokes that he took and the other did not, which golfer do you think would have the least number of strokes and therefore win the game? Obviously, the man who counted his strokes, because it provided him with a way of measuring himself, and a way of challenging himself to better performance.

Experience—
How to Get the Right Kind

M ANY BELIEVE that if you took all the money away from the rich people and gave it to the poor people, it would not be long before the people who formerly had the money would have all of it back. We have also heard that when a man with experience deals with a man who has money, the man with experience ends up with the money and the other man gets the experience.

What is the point? It is simply that, as the old cliche tells us, "there is no substitute for experience." But this really isn't the whole story. The implication in there being no substitute for experience is, that the only way you can get experience is to put in the time. This is only one of *three* ways to get experience. It also happens to be the hardest way to get experience. Unfortunately, many people who think that they have gained ten or twenty years of experience have actually had only one year of experience ten or twenty times. They have experienced no personal growth.

The three ways to get experience are:
1. Put in the time.
2. Read.
3. Listen and talk to others.

The best way to get experience from the standpoint of return on investment in your time is by reading. The really great thing about reading to gain experience is that you can get it *any time* you want it, *any place* you want to get it, from *anyone* you wish (living or dead). Reading enables you to communicate with the all-time greats in any field.

Books are great treasures and public libraries are fine, particularly for browsing through books. However, the purchase of good books is one of the finest investments you can make. Furthermore, regardless of what you may have been taught in public school, you should *write* in your books—mark them up. It is difficult for me to read a book without a ballpoint pen in my hand to underline passages of particular interest and perhaps jot comments or ideas in the margins. I often go back and browse through my books taking particular note of the underlined passages and comments that I have made.

Another excellent way of gaining experience without putting in a long period of time is by listening and talking with others. This way you can vicariously gain the experience that others have gained. It also has the advantage over reading in that you can have two-way communication. You can ask questions and get answers back. You are in a conversational "mode" (as they say in the computer business.)

A WORD OF WARNING ABOUT GAINING EXPERIENCE VICARIOUSLY THROUGH OTHERS—it is a fact of human nature in many people that they will give you advice even if they do not know what they are talking about. They are self-appointed experts on any subject: government, sports, business, you name it.

A few years ago, I visited Cape Cod for the first time. On Saturday morning, I stopped off in Plymouth to get a haircut. In talking with the barber I told him that I had time to go to either Nantucket Island or Martha's Vineyard. Which of the two islands would he recommend? He said that by all means I should go to Martha's Vineyard; and he then spent several minutes extolling the virtues of that island and telling of his experiences there. I then asked him how much time he had spent on Nantucket Island, to which he replied, "Oh, I've never been to Nantucket!" We must qualify those from whom we seek to learn. Perhaps they give us advice although "they have never been to Nantucket." (Incidentally, I went to Nantucket. I still haven't been to Martha's Vineyard.)

Perhaps we gain our greatest experience from failure and adversity. It is not the most pleasant way to gain experience but it is often the way that we get our most lasting experience. We must discipline ourselves to look on failure as a learning process and to not become discouraged and "overlearn" from experience.

> Any one who has had a long life of experiences is worth listening to, worth emulating, and worth tying to as a friend. No one can have too much experience in any line of endeavor. We readily welcome to our group of friends that one who talks with the voice of experience and common sense. We know that we are safe in his hands. He is not going to get us into trouble. Rather he is going to point out the pitfalls and mistakes that experience has taught him to avoid. There is no experience but what carries its lasting good for us along with it. And you don't have to discard experience. It's a coat for life! It never wears out.
>
> —George Matthew Adams

■ Failure Is a Learning Process

> Failure is, in a sense, the highway to success, inasmuch as every discovery of what is false leads us to seek earnestly after what is true.
> —John Keats

No one likes to fail at anything, but you might as well accept the fact that an integral part of being successful is a healthy ration of failure. Failing and losing does not make you a "loser" unless you let it affect you that way. You should assume the attitude that if you ever want to really accomplish anything it will involve some risk, and with risk there is the very real possibility of various degrees of failure. We should view failure positively from the standpoint of what it has taught us.

Someone once said that history is prologue. Everything that has happened in the past is the beginning of where we go from here. If you dismiss the lessons of failure from your mind and do not look for the positive benefits, you are passing by perhaps THE greatest learning vehicle. Success is great, but when things are going our way, the lessons of success often do not leave imprints in our minds to the extent that the lessons of failure do.

Thomas Edison conducted thousands of experiments before he developed the electric light. One of his associates, who was rather discouraged at one point, was told by Edison, "Look at how much we have learned from our failures. We know about thousands of things that will not work." By the process of elimination, by learning from what would not work, they became successful.

I have failed many times in business. The first business I ever got into involved putting coin-operated radios in hospitals. I failed at that and it cost me $2000 which was a hell of a lot of money to me then (and it still is.) I then failed in the upholstering business. Although the company that I have been running for over fourteen years has been successful, I have failed several times in new areas. I failed when we tried to start a blueprinting service. I failed when we tried to start a microfilming service. The reason that you do not hear more about the failures of successful people and successful businesses is that they are usually kept as quiet as possible. It is damaging to the ego. As I have read the biographies of great men and organizations, I have been impressed by the fact that some degree of failure has been common to almost all of them.

Failure in organizations knows no bounds. It hits the large as well as the small. Fortunately for the larger corporations, they can cope with failure more easily than can small undercapitalized companies. How many companies, for example, could afford to lose approximately $350,000,000 as Ford Motor Company did on the Edsel? We find this to be true also of individuals. Some people are much better prepared to take a severe loss than are others. For this reason, I would remind you that the "Early Christians got all of the hungry lions." At times, without the resources to wait out a possible storm, people will want to jump in on the start of a brand new idea or venture, even though it has not been tried or proven at all in the marketplace. You do not have to be the *first* in most things to be successful. You can be *one of the first*—and still be highly successful. There were many people who waited for the start of a good track record in IBM, Polaroid, and Xerox before getting on the bandwagon and they still made fortunes.

It is not logical to assume that what has worked once will necessarily work again. It is equally illogical to assume that just because we have failed in one type of situation, the same approach will not work in a different situation. Unfortunately, we sometimes *over*learn from experience. We fail at something and we give up. Mark Twain said, "If a cat sits on a hot stove, he will never sit on a hot stove again. BUT, he won't sit on a cold stove either." The cat just gets out of the business of sitting on stoves. The cat has overlearned from experience. Aren't we the same way at times? The object is to learn from failure, not to "overlearn" from failure.

Whenever we make a decision to embark on an uncharted course, no matter how optimistic we may be as to the outcome, we should discipline ourselves to always ask the questions: What is the very worst that can happen? What is my maximum exposure? What conditions would have to exist in order to indicate that the new project is a failure? It is said that the most unrealistic person is a pessimist. A person who makes decisions without risk assessments may be optimistic, but he is hardly realistic.

We should not "fear" failure. We should "respect" failure. When we operate in an environment of fear we become emotional and lose our objectivity. We are inhibited in expressing ourselves. We become reluctant to delegate any of the responsibility to others for fear that they will fail and we will become a part of their failure.

We should study our failures seriously and objectively and

perhaps bring in someone with an unbiased viewpoint to help analyze them. We have a tendency to excuse the factors in our failures that are functions of our own personal actions. It is too easy when things turn out well to assume it was because of our ability, and when things don't turn out well to blame it on the circumstances. As you study your failures, you should carefully document in writing what you have learned. You should write it down, because the human memory has a wonderful faculty for erasing the unpleasantness of the past. The psychologists call this "repression." We tend to remember what we want to remember, our successes and our pleasant experiences, not our failures. This mental process however works against us in attempting to learn *lasting* lessons from our failures, unless we do make written notes.

Failure is a matter of degree. Some failures are major; others amount to nothing more than disappointments. People who develop a psychological "hang-up" about not wanting to accept failure are heading for sure trouble. They are very likely to end up in a situation where they will fight to the death instead of taking a mild, temporary defeat and giving it another "go" later. There is a lot of wisdom in the old saying "He who fights and runs away, lives to fight another day." Discretion is not "quitting."

If you play poker you know the value of this lesson. In poker you take a lot of small defeats while awaiting your chance. Then, when you know that you have the right cards, you wage battle on a full scale. It takes patience and good timing. But if you get emotional and begin to inflate the value of your cards, you may end up fighting to the death.

There was once a man who had ample opportunity to learn from failure as his track record would indicate:

In 1831—He failed in business
    1832—Was defeated for the legislature
    1833—Failed in business again
    1834—Elected to the legislature
    1835—His sweetheart died
    1836—Had a nervous breakdown

1838—Defeated for speaker
1840—Defeated for elector
1843—Defeated for congress
1846—Elected to congress
1848—Defeated for congress
1855—Defeated for senate
1856—Defeated for vice-president of the United States
1858—Defeated for senate
1860—Elected president of the United States.

What was his name? Abraham Lincoln.

Similarly Richard Nixon suffered many defeats in his rise to the Presidency.

Thomas J. Watson, the founder of IBM, was no stranger to failure. Watson had run afoul of the antitrust laws and at forty years of age had been fired as the sales manager of the National Cash Register Company. As it was expressed in *The Lengthening Shadow* by Belden, (about Watson), "At forty he seemed a failure; disgraced, under jail sentence, with no job, no home, little money. And what success he had achieved in the past was modest."

Life is a series of experiences, each one of which makes us bigger, even though sometimes it is hard to realize this. For the world was built to develop character, and we must learn that the setbacks and griefs which we endure help us in our marching onward.

—Henry Ford

■ Bumblebees *Can* Fly

Nothing will ever be attempted if all possible objections must be first overcome.

—Samuel Johnson

They say that a group of aeronautical engineers studied the bumblebee and concluded that because of its wing span, body shape, weight, etc., the bumblebee CANNOT fly. The bumblebee, however, does not know that he cannot fly, so he flies anyhow. I am glad that when I went into business I did not know as much as I do now or perhaps I would not have gone into business. I would have known too many reasons why I would not make it. I did not know any better so I flew anyhow. It is a case of the depth of a man's convictions overcoming the height of the logic that tells you not to embark on a specific project.

> Progress in every age results only from the fact that there are some men and women who refuse to believe that what they knew to be right cannot be done.
>
> —Russell W. Davenport

Whenever you consider taking on a challenge—something a little above the "norm," something that has not been tried before, a new approach to something that has been around awhile—you find that many people do not think it is a good idea. The reason is obvious; if your idea was of the "can't miss" type, a real cinch with no element of uncertainty, you can bet that someone else would have already done it.

> Some men see things as they are and ask, "Why?" I dream things that never were and ask, "why not?"
>
> —Robert F. Kennedy

People who display creative thinking and come up with ideas that really click have to be practical and visionary all at the same time. You have to be able to dream, but at the same time be able to conceive of a way that the dream can be fulfilled. You can sit around and dream big dreams of building an empire with a chain of shoeshine parlors, but unless you can think of a practical plan for doing it, it will remain only an impossible dream. Dreaming does not make you a "dreamer" unless your dream is really "An Impossible Dream."

I believe in the type of dreaming Conrad Hilton refers to in his book *Be My Guest*:

> There's enthusiasm, and finding your talent, and a lot of other things that go to make up successful living. . . . This was the missing piece. *You had to dream.*

The type of dreaming that appeals to me has nothing to do with a reverie, an idle daydream. It isn't wishful thinking. Nor is it the type of revelation reserved for the great ones and rightly called vision. What I speak of is a brand of imaginative thinking backed by enthusiasm, vitality, expectation to which all men may aspire.

To accomplish big things I am convinced you must first dream big dreams. True, it must be in line with progress, human and divine, or you are wasting your prayer. It has to be backed by work and faith, or it has no hands and feet. Maybe there's even an element of luck mixed in. But I am sure now that, without this master plan, you have nothing.

My own dreams were smaller than some—bigger than others. Some had flaws in them and fell apart before they could take form. Others were misguided; the energy behind them had to be redirected according to a sounder plan. . . .

A classic example of this would be in the case of Holiday Inns. In the early days they had a difficult time selling a new concept for the motel business. Motels had been around for a long time and this new concept represented a radical departure from that to which people had been accustomed.

Seek out advice, but do so with the realization that you very likely will get more negative than positive reactions, particularly from those who might have some sort of a "stake" in what you want to do. This could represent potential investors, bankers, creditors, employees, etc. People who do not have such a "stake" will more than likely take the easy way out and tell you that they think you have a good idea whether they think so or not.

Dreamers and doers—the world generally divides men into these two general classifications, but the world is often wrong. There are men who win the admiration and respect of their fellowmen. They are the men worthwhile. Dreaming is just another name for thinking, planning, devising—another way of saying that a man exercises his soul. A steadfast soul, holding steadily to a dream ideal, plus a sturdy will determined to succeed in any venture, can make any dream come true. Use your mind and you will. They work together for you beautifully if you'll only give them a chance.

—B. N. Mills

■ **Mentally Move from Washington Street**

To every man his chance, to every man, regardless of his birth, his shining golden opportunity. To every man the right to live, to work, to be himself, and to become whatever thing his manhood and his vision can contribute to make him.

—Thomas Wolfe

When I was a child I lived on the north side of Atlanta until I was in the second grade at which time, because of my father's illness, I went to live with my grandparents on Washington Street, which is on the south side of the city. In the early nineteen hundreds when my grandparents bought their house, Washington Street was a very fashionable street. However, it later became somewhat run down and by the time I went to live there it was a very poor neighborhood. Two years later, my father died and my mother and I moved into an apartment again on the north side of Atlanta in a very nice neighborhood. I went to school with children from middle and upper income families as opposed to the children from the lower income families on the south side.

In later years, I would occasionally run into some of those with whom I had gone to school on the south side. I do not know where they were physically living at the time, but I do know that too many of them were still mentally living on Washington Street. They had not raised their sights above what they had seen in their Washington Street environment.

I did not like living on Washington Street—but in retrospect I would not take anything for the experience. Having lived there and afterward having moved to the north side gave me a basis of comparison. It spurred me on to make sure that, if it were my preference to remain on the north side, I could do so. Joe E. Lewis said "I've been rich and I've been poor. Rich is better." I was not necessarily looking to be rich, but I sure as hell wanted to stay away from Washington Street.

Even those who grow up in an atmosphere of affluence often mentally are living on Washington Street. They put a ceiling on themselves. They decide that they are able to do only so much and that is it. This is even more likely to happen to a man who grows up poor. He looks at his father who makes $600 per month; and as soon as *he gets* to $650 a month he says: "I make more than my old man does and that's pretty good." By using his father as a standard he has put a very low limit on what he thinks he can accomplish.

It is a matter of attitude and perspective. It is too easy for a person from the "wrong side of the tracks" to assume the role of the downtrodden or the "underdog." We are what our thoughts make us. If we decide that we are the underdogs, that is what we will become. Mike Todd, the great showman, said, "I have been broke many times, but I have never been poor." This is a marvelous attitude. "Poor" is a state of the mind. If you come from Washington Street, you should look for the positive trade offs. It is a great experience. It should spur you on to get you out of that environment. It gives you perspective in that once you begin to achieve success it will make you appreciate what you have accomplished more than would be the case if you had always been accustomed to having everything you wanted. Living on Washington Street makes you a "scrapper" who knows the meaning of hard work. It enables you to learn to communicate effectively with the masses which is a *must* if you do want to be successful.

> All of us have imagined limitations, but we have also the privilege of pushing them aside, and spreading our lives out!
>
> —George Matthew Adams

> When a man has put a limit on what he will do, he has put a limit on what he can do.
>
> —Charles M. Schwab

■ Ignore Competition at Your Peril

> Next to knowing all about your own business, the best thing is to know all about the other fellow's business.
>
> —John D. Rockefeller

Recently I heard what I consider to be a rather asinine radio editorial in which the radio reporter was suggesting to people that they should ignore their competition and instead concentrate all of their efforts on "doing their own thing." This reporter used the example of a well-known professional golfer who was quoted as saying that he ignored his competition and instead concentrated on his own game. Golf is not a very good analogy for the types of competition with which most people are confronted. However, even in golf the pros do not ignore their competition.

Competition is the name of the game in the United States. We live in a competitive society. The first games that we learn when we are kids are competitive in nature. All through schools we are graded on a competitive basis and we engage in competitive sports. We enter business and are thrown into a competitive environment. We meet outside competition. Within the organization we compete with each other in our rise to the top. Competition is all about us. Telling a person to ignore competition is like telling fish to ignore the water.

Don't fear competition; respect it. Give competition the benefit of the doubt and assume that you do not have a monopoly on brains or a better way to accomplish an objective. Competition represents one of your best vehicles for learning. To ignore competition is to ignore a prime source for development.

By studying your competition, you may find a major key to success. A great many people and businesses have become successful by observing the good and bad things that the competition were doing and then picking out or improving upon the things that were good. Studying competition often gives you the spark of an idea that will apply in a somewhat unrelated area.

As to our golfer friend who allegedly ignored his competition, does he still play with clubs that have wooden shafts? Somewhere along the line he may have observed that his competition is playing with clubs that had steel shafts. When he is in a tournament, does he ignore the scores of his competitors? When faced with a 12-foot putt on the eighteenth, does he know whether or not he must sink it to win?

There are thousands of instances where businessmen have observed competition and have improved their own products. We see it everywhere—in automobiles, aerosol cans, plastic containers instead of glass containers, "six-packs" and on and on. And there are thousands of instances where businessmen ignored competition—and lost out.

When you don't know your competition you overlook one of the most effective means of selling your ideas—competitive selling. Competitive selling does not mean "blasting" your competition. You should never run down the competition. The comparison should be made on a positive note. Our car costs more, but the trade-in value will be much higher in three years. We give less gas mileage, but offer more comfort at a little extra cost. They give faster service, but we can save you money. Having something to measure your product against effectively makes it easier to sell and makes it easier for the prospect to buy.

Competition is healthy. It stimulates us to do better than we would otherwise—and gives us tips on *how* we can do better.

People seldom improve when they have no other model but themselves to copy after.

—Goldsmith

Failure-Avoiders
and Success-Seekers—
The Traps on the
Road Upward

You will never stub your toe standing still. The faster you go, the
more chance there is of stubbing your toe, but the more chance you
have of getting somewhere.

—Charles F. Kettering

THERE ARE MILLIONS of failure-avoiders. While they do not
represent any competition to those who are seeking success,
it is important that the success-seeker identify these people. "No
man is an island" when it comes to being successful. A successful
person almost always finds his success interrelated with the success of other people who seek success. But if you are surrounded
by people who are merely avoiding failure, you could become an
"island" without realizing it. Let's examine the characteristics of
failure-avoiders and how they affect success-seekers.

Failure-avoiders are often difficult to detect because many of
them work very hard. They are working very hard to avoid fail-

ure. This is their goal. They do not think in terms of failure and success. *They think in terms of failure and the avoidance of failure.* They will only strive for those goals that represent no real risk.

You cannot assume from this that failure-avoiders are not found in high places. On the contrary, they often get quite high up in the organization for a very good reason. In some large organizations, as in government service, steady, reliable performance can be more important than showing creative initiative or drive. These people are not victims of the "Peter Principle." They have not reached a "level of inefficiency." They are usually over qualified for the job that they are doing and they like it that way. They quietly fight being promoted into a position where they will be challenged or put into the limelight.

You lose your perspective about many of these people because they are such "nice guys." Everybody likes them. Why not? They don't "rattle the cage." They don't want to make waves. They want to keep things as they are. They are easy to get along with in a meeting, never get involved in disputes and are not thought of as threats to their fellow employee. These are the ways that they "insulate" their own security.

After reading about failure-avoiders you may conclude that you do not see anything wrong with this posture. Well, that is for you to decide, but this book is not written for those avoiding failure. It is written for those who want to make something happen, who are seeking success, who want to capitalize on opportunities. Let's examine how failure-avoiders impact success.

Here is a quotation from Peter Drucker in his book *Managing For Results.* (In my estimation, this is the best book that I have read on business philosophy.)

Results are obtained by exploiting opportunities, not by solving problems. All one can hope to get by solving a problem is to restore normality. . . . Resources, to produce results, must be allocated to opportunities, rather then to problems. Needless to say, one cannot shrug off all problems, but they can and should be minimized. "Maximization of opportunities" is a meaningful, indeed a precise, definition of the entreprenurial job. . . . It is futile to restore normality; "normal ity" is only the reality of yesterday. The job is not to impose yesterday's normal on a changed today; but to change the business, its behavior, its attitudes, its expectations . . . to fit the new realities.

Drucker states the challenge very well. The failure-avoiders are concerned with solving problems in order to get things back to normal, the way they were yesterday. They try to restore the status quo, for in doing so they are attempting to avoid the risk of failure that is an integral part of seeking success. Failure-avoiders seek competence, but it is through *leadership* that results are obtained. Drucker points out the folly of trying to restore yesterday's norm to a changed today. John Shedd pointed out that: "A ship in harbor is safe, but that is not what ships are built for."

The success-seekers on the other hand are "making it happen." They are interested in the future, not in the past, and in exploiting opportunity, not solving problems except to a minimum degree. They know that results are not obtained by competence but by displaying leadership.

There's no thrill in easy sailing when the skies are clear and blue, there's no joy in merely doing things which any one can do. But there is some satisfaction that is mighty sweet to take, when you reach a destination that you thought you'd never make.

—Spirella

▪ Don't Put Yourself in the "Work" Prison

The person who studiously avoids work usually works far harder that the man who pleasantly confronts it and does it. Men who cannot work are not happy men.

—L. Ron Hubbard

I will never forget a conversation I had a long time ago with a widowed lady in a small southern town that had a population of less than one thousand. She indicated one of the regrets she had about her husband was that he had never really gotten to know their children when they were growing up because he had spent so much time working in a local business. To me, the irony of the situation was that you could look out of the window of his business and see the house in which he had lived and in which his children had grown up. It was also ironic to me that here, in this sleepy little town, the picture of peace and tranquility, this man had apparently created a "work" prison for himself. You can live and work in the middle of the largest city in the world and be less of a prisoner than you might be in a very small town with less than a thousand people.

It all gets back to *attitude*. It is through our attitude that we put ourselves in work prisons. Business is not a jungle unless you see it as such. (The same is true of a large city. I once lived next door to a couple who announced one day that they were tired of the "rat race" in Atlanta and were going to move to Wyoming and "get away from it all." Shortly thereafter, they had found another rat race in Wyoming and were anxious to get back to Atlanta.) The rat race is created by a mental, not a physical, environment.

Work is a privilege and should be viewed as such. Remember, the last day you will ever "work" will be the day you fall in love with what it is that you are doing.

An article in the July 1969 issue of *Look* magazine concerned two American prisoners of the Red Chinese. The biggest complaint one of these prisoners had was that the Red Chinese would not let him do any work. The Red Chinese are masters of psychological torture and I am sure that it was very much by design that they deprived the prisoners of work. Finally, the Chinese allowed the men to sweep up their compound and the article relates how much it meant to these prisoners to be able to do any kind of work again. This is a pretty tough way to learn the value of being able to work. Many people work for years in order that they can retire only to find upon retirement that what they really enjoyed was the work that they did, not the retirement.

We seldom realize how much we enjoy anything until after we have had an opportunity to look back on it in retrospect. As I look back on the last eighteen years that I spent first with the

IBM Corporation and then with Management Services, Inc., I begin to get the full impact of how much it has meant to me. I sometimes have a daydream that I would like to go back and do it all over again starting from zero. However, it would not be the same as it was the first time. Although I could start without any financial resources, I would still have had the experience which is more valuable than the financial resources, and it was in gaining the experience that I derived a major part of the satisfaction.

It is not true that you have to make great sacrifices to be successful. This in itself is a contradiction. Sacrifice means "to suffer loss of, give up, renounce, injure or destroy for an end." How can you feel that you are achieving success if you have to endure what sacrifice implies. The "game would not be worth the candle," The game *is* worth the candle. What you invest (not sacrifice) in the way of time and effort pays off manyfold in the way of return.

> The law of work does not seem utterly fair—but there it is, and nothing can change it; the higher the pay in enjoyment the worker gets out of it, the higher shall be his pay in money also.
>
> —Mark Twain

▪ Hours in Gethsemane

> They came to a place called Gethsemane . . . and he began to feel distress and dread, and he said to them, "My heart is almost breaking". . . . And he went on a little way and threw himself on the ground and prayed that if it were possible he might be spared the hour of trial.
> Mark 14:32–35

Very few successful men have not spent a great deal of time "In Gethsemane"—very deep trouble. It is during adversity that the men are separated from the boys—"when the going gets tough, the tough get going." After the attack on Pearl Harbor a Japanese admiral said: "I fear that we have awakened a sleeping giant with terrible resolve." How right he was. The United

States had gotten somewhat soft, but it rallied in the face of adversity during its hours in Gethsemane.

How many highly successful men would be that way if they had not been put to the test? It gets back again to succeeding in spite of yourself. You do what you *want* to do or *have* to do. When we face crisis, we are often called on to do that which we did not think we could do. Once the experience is behind us, we realize that we were challenged and we met the challenge. We then upgrade our self-image and become better able to use the abilities and the capacities that were already there. In this respect we have changed. Men who have never had to react to a crisis have no real way of measuring themselves. They have no basis of comparison between what they do and what they are capable of doing.

It is like running the four-minute mile. Once it was established that it could be done, it became almost commonplace. The capacity was always there, but the mental barrier had to be broken before the physical barrier could be overcome. As in the case of the four-minute milers, we sometime walk around with much more capacity than we could possibly imagine that we have.

The amount of adversity in successful careers is not well publicized for obvious reasons. Successful people accept adversity as the norm and are interested in the NET results of their achievements, less their setbacks.

Adversity does more than increase your awareness of your abilities and capacities. You also begin to build up a certain immunity to trouble. It all becomes relative. You get to the point that you say to yourself, "Well, I'm in hot water again. So what else is new?" This is not an invitation to ignore trouble, but rather to learn to cope with it. If you have too much trouble you can get wiped out in the process—like the man who was about to be hanged and said, "This is going to be a good lesson for me."

If there is ever a time when you need to maintain your perspective and a positive attitude it is in the face of adversity. It is not difficult to maintain a positive attitude when everything is going your way.

The difficulties, hardships and trials of life, the obstacles one encounters on the road to fortune are positive blessings. They knit the muscles more firmly, and teach self-reliance. Peril is the element in which power is developed.

—W. Mathews

■ I'm Wrong. So What!

One of the major reasons for failure is the inability of a great number of people to admit that they have been wrong, have made a mistake or have failed.

Perhaps the most common characteristic among great business leaders is that at one time or another they all seem to have experienced a major failure. (J. C. Penney, Thomas J. Watson of IBM, Conrad Hilton, etc.; and nonbusinessmen such as Abraham Lincoln and Richard Nixon.)

If I were to plot the mistakes that I have made and the times that I have been wrong on a sheet of graph paper, it would probably show that I have had a rather continuous record of having been wrong about something almost all of the time. If this is true, it is logical to assume that after twenty-one years I will not suddenly begin to be right all of the time and that if I plot this graph into the future I will have a lot more mistakes ahead of me.

Being wrong a great deal of the time should not cause you to develop a negative attitude. On the contrary, you should maintain a positive attitude. The recognition that being wrong is very natural, should fortify your belief in yourself and help you to maintain a positive outlook in spite of frequent failures. There is a lot of difference in having lost and being a "loser." You are a loser when you can not cope with failure.

Failure should spur you on, not tear you down. The only way I know of to keep from being wrong is to never make any decisions. You must learn to live with the fact that the more decisions you make, the more times you are going to be wrong. What counts is the net result of your successes and failures. Mickey

Mantle had an unusually high number of strike outs, but he is not remembered for the number of times he failed at the plate but instead for the number of times that he was successful in hitting the ball.

■ The Blind Men and the Elephant

One principal reason why men are so useless is, that they divide and shift their attention among a multiplicity of objects and pursuits.

—Emmons

Four blind men were led up to an elephant without being told what the object was. Each blind man was asked to put his hand on the object and describe what it was that he felt. The first blind man put his hand on the elephant's side and said he felt a wall. The second blind man put his hand on the elephant's leg and said he felt a tree trunk. The third blind man put his hand on the elephant's tail and said he felt a rope. The other blind man put his hand on the elephant's trunk and said he felt a fire hose.

Many people in organizations are like the blind men. They become so highly specialized and concentrate on what THEY are doing to such a degree that they develop nearsightedness about the rest of the business. They have no idea of the overall thrust of the business; they begin to mistake their corner of the room for the whole building.

The trend in American business is more and more toward specialization. I agree with Peter Drucker:

Concentration is the key to economic results. Economic results require that managers concentrate their efforts on the smallest number of activities that will produce the largest amount of revenue. . . . Human resources must be concentrated on a few major opportunities. . . . No other principle is violated as constantly today as the basic principle of concentration. . . . Our motto seems to be "Let's do a little bit of everything."

Specialization, however, can be carried too far. There is an old saying that "A one-eyed man is king in the land of the blind."

You do not have to be an expert in all facets of your organization. This would not be possible. But, like the "one-eyed man," and unlike the men around the elephant, you should not be completely blind to the environment around you.

The point is that while you specialize, you must maintain flexibility in your thinking and at the same time be constantly aware of your surroundings. This is essential unless you want to leave your success to chance. There are too many instances where businesses and individuals have disregarded the fact that the world was changing around them only to wake up one day with the horrible realization that they had become obsolete. As the pace of life and business continues to accelerate, it becomes increasingly more important that we remain aware of our surroundings.

When I was a boy, there was a company in Atlanta called the Atlantic Ice and Coal Company. They sold blocks of ice for ice boxes in the home. They also sold coal, primarily for use in stoves and fireplaces. I cannot think of two products that could have had a more dismal outlook for the future back in the 1930's. I am not really familiar with the details of the company, but I do know that as time passed they converted their choice business locations from ice and coal houses to convenience grocery stores. Instead of continuing to concentrate on selling ice by the block they began to sell crushed ice in bags as party ice. The company subsequently went through some name changes and mergers, but today is alive and well. This certainly seems to be a case of an organization being aware of the surroundings while specializing.

Thomas J. Watson was quoted as having said he was only smart in spots, but he stuck to those spots. IBM is another example of a company that was highly specialized, concentrating on producing punched card accounting machines. Punched card accounting machines built the business for over forty years before computers ever came on the scene. IBM, however, was aware of the surroundings and saw the "handwriting on the wall" with the result that they got into the computer business. They were not the first to enter this field, but they now have approximately seventy percent of the market.

The area around Vernal, Utah, is popularly called "Dinosaur-land," for it is in this area that some of the largest known deposits of dinosaur fossils in the world have been found. Apparently these dinosaurs were born, lived and died in this small area. As you know, they were very large animals and they had hearty appetites although they were vegetarians. When finally all of the vegetation in the area had been consumed, the dinosaurs starved to death because they were not able to adapt themselves to their environment and move on to other areas.

Chameleons on the other hand, have been with us since the age of the dinosaurs and have survived very well. They are extremely flexible in that their eyeballs move independently of each other and can spot an approaching enemy. They also have the ability to change their colors to adapt to their surroundings, making them very difficult to see. They have a keen sense of smell and can literally taste odors in the air by constantly flicking their tongues.

Businesses and people are like dinosaurs and chameleons. Some do not adapt to the environment and die out like the dinosaurs. Others are like the chameleons. They adapt to the environment and do very well. Our challenge is to become more like the chameleons and less like the dinosaurs.

Business history has proven that industries, individual businesses, and individual jobs go through a life cycle of birth, infancy, maturity, old age and finally death. This is not an inevitable process; the life cycle can often be extended indefinitely by adapting to changing conditions. You should always be aware of the current status of your industry, your business and your individual job for any signs that you should take steps to adapt to the changing environment. Many salesmen have learned too late that selling styles have gone through an evolution that puts in serious jeopardy the backslapping, joke telling, "good-time Charlie" type of salesman of the past. Today's typical salesman sells solutions to problems rather than products. He is more technically oriented and tends to sell a system for doing a job even when there is a product involved. The product has become a means to an end, a vehicle for solving a specific problem rather than an end in itself.

Limiting one's pursuits to one lone avenue without benefit of change or diversion can result in a form of vapidity which sometimes deadens imagination.

—Edwin G. Uhl

■ Beware the Rapture of the Heights

Success has ruin'd many a man.

—Benjamin Franklin

There is a phenomenon known as the "rapture of the deep." Swimmers who have dived to great depths experience a chemical reaction in the blood stream which gives them an intoxicating feeling of great exhilaration. When this occurs they may dive much deeper than the human body can withstand. Swimmers have been known to pull off their artificial lungs as they go deeper to certain death.

The dictionary defines "rapture" as a state or experience of being carried away by overwhelming emotion. It is SHOCKING, in studying the lives of businessmen, to discover the great number of times that they experience what I call the "rapture of the heights." This is the state or experience of being carried away by the overwhelming emotion of the pinnacle of success. The result is often crisis and failure. Many of us are alumni of that great fraternity of the "rapture of the heights."

In the poem "IF" Rudyard Kipling refers to many things that will make a man of you, including:

If you can make one heap of all your winnings
and risk it on one turn of pitch-and-toss,
and lose, and start again at your beginnings,
and never breathe a word about your loss etc., etc.

Mr. Kipling is right. It will make a man out of you, but that is doing it the hard way. When he says "and never breathe a word about your loss," this is the easy part. No one likes to admit that he has been an idiot. Unfortunately, this is what many of us have been. We enjoy a little success and all of a sudden we think that we can do no wrong. Instead of continuing to take *risks*, (the possibility of loss), we begin to take *chances*. The dictionary tells us that *chance* "involves things that happen unpredictably without intention or cause." Mr. Kipling calls it "pitch-and-toss"; nowadays we would call it shooting "craps" with our lives.

The irony is that the rapture of the heights normally takes place after we have reached a point of diminishing returns on what we could gain by continuing. Men who "have it made" and would never have to work again will lay it all on the line in order to achieve more success. This is one of the potential disadvantages of success-seeking. The very things that make a man successful are the same things that make him achieve more and more success. As my friend, Marshall J. Mantler, so wisely pointed out to me: "The more successful we become, the more we demand of ourselves."

I have had many personal experiences with rapture of the heights. Here is a classic:

In June 1965, I invested (I use the word loosely) $12,000 in wheat futures in the commodity market. By December 31 of the same year, without putting in any more money, I had $93,000 in my commodity account. I couldn't believe it, and I was frustrated that the commodity market had been in existence for so long without my taking advantage of it and cashing in on this "gravy train." I started running all sorts of analyses on the computer as to what the action of the commodity market was signifying in the way of price actions in the future. But the market did not respond as I thought it was *supposed to*. The sad ending to the story is that by June 1966, almost a year to the day after I had gotten into the market, I had lost my $81,000 profit plus my original investment of $12,000. It was a case, pure and simple, of the rapture of the heights. I was intoxicated with my success and had gone way beyond the point of diminishing returns when considering the tax consequences of the additional profits that I could have made. Instead of taking risks, I began to take chances.

For those readers who also happen to be my creditors, it is with a certain amount of trepidation that I recount my experiences in the commodity market. Remember, however, that "no one is as moral as a reformed whore." I've learned my lesson.

The message in this chapter is that if you do not fall victim to this emotion as you achieve degrees of success, you will be in the minority. It is something that you should guard against. People *do* get wiped out in the success process, never to make a comeback, while others come back stronger than ever. It's good experience, but very expensive. I have read that quick success and quick failure is the American cult of the failure of success.

You—
Your Job—
and Your Boss

To find a career to which you are adapted by nature, and then to work hard at it, is about as near to a formula for success and happiness as the world provides. One of the fortunate aspects of this formula is that, granted the right career has been found, the hard work takes care of itself. Then hard work is not hard work at all.

—Mark Sullivan

SOMEONE ONCE SAID that a diamond was only a piece of coal that stuck with it. Similarly, big businesses are only little businesses that grew up. Most people are amazingly arbitrary about choosing an organization with which to work. They display blind faith that if they work hard they will automatically progress in the organization. As the song says "It Ain't Necessarily So." The industry in which a company operates may not have much of a future; and any given company, regardless of the outlook for the industry, may not be going any place.

Here are some fundamentals for choosing the best affiliation for *you*:

1. Get in an industry that is almost sure to grow faster than the Gross National Product. There is much information from the government and other sources that makes this determination quite simple.

2. Determine the industry which appears to be the most interesting to you and then select companies within the industry that should grow faster than the industry itself. Now you have increased the odds of success: you are looking at companies that should grow faster than their industry, and whose industry should grow faster than the Gross National Product.

3. Make a decision as to the size company you would like to work with. You may want to work with one of the giant corporations or a smaller organization, or you may want to start your own business.

I lean toward smaller organizations after having worked for several different sized companies including IBM, which does over eight billion dollars per year in sales. I favor smaller organizations for the following reasons:

a. You get much better potential leverage. Obviously, a company doing two million in sales has a much better chance of growing percentage-wise much faster than IBM would for example with an eight billion dollar sales base. A two million dollar company might grow two hundred percent to six million in sales with relative ease compared to what IBM would have to do to show much of a percentage increase in their growth.

b. You have a much higher degree of visibility and impact in a small company. If you have "something on the ball," it becomes a lot more obvious in a smaller company where everyone has a much greater impact on the progress of the company. In the case of a much larger organization with thousands of employees there is an inherent danger of getting lost in the shuffle no matter how sharp you are. You might also become a victim of circumstances and get "shot down" by a manager with whom you do not have a good working relationship.

However, if you are certain you definitely have limited ability, you should join a large organization. You *will not be* so highly visible; but more importantly, you will stand a good chance of getting into some kind of highly specialized work in which you can excel. One characteristic of most small businesses is that you MUST have a high degree of versatility and flexibility in order to wear the many hats that are necessary and be able to "keep a lot of balloons in the air" at the same time.

c. You can see the big picture more easily in a small company. In a large organization there is a tendency for people to begin to mistake their corner of the building for the whole business. They often lose sight of the business that they are really in and become very much "inside-focused."

d. It is much easier to identify your personal objectives with those of the smaller organization. Compatibility of objectives between the individual and the organization is a MUST if you want to be successful.

e. In a smaller company, you can evaluate the management more easily. Regardless of the industry and its bright outlook and regardless of the reputation the organization might have enjoyed in the *past*, the future of a firm is going to be determined to a very large degree by the ability of the management of the company. As Peter Drucker says: "Knowledge is the only real distinct resource that one business can have over another." This knowledge and the application of knowledge by the management of the company is all important.

f. Smaller companies are much more flexible than larger companies. They can change the direction of the company and "go where the action is." It is a more dynamic environment in that the company can respond to current conditions without being hindered by their size.

g. There is a much greater opportunity for making a LOT of money in a smaller business. I am convinced, based on my experience, that there are many more millionaires per capita in businesses doing one to twenty-five million dollars in annual sales than in the *Fortune* 500 list of the largest companies in the United States.

Admitting at the outset that I have a prejudice against large corporations, I will attempt to eliminate my bias and list the advantages of going with a larger corporation.

a. The big organization usually has a much higher degree of permanence . . . although this does not necessarily spell more security for the individual.

b. Training is done on a more professional basis and is likely to be much better than you could find in a smaller company.

c. There is more evidence of professional management as opposed to intuitive "flying by the seat of the pants."

d. The big company is less susceptible to nepotism.

e. The large organization is better for people who want to work in staff or highly specialized types of work.

f. Bigness accommodates the nonmavericks who like to work in a formalized structure.

g. The large company is the best environment for people who don't make things happen. Someone once said that people can be divided into three groups:

1. Those who make something happen.

2. Those who watch others make something happen.

3. Those who don't know what's happening.

If you fall into categories 2 or 3, you definitely should work for a "biggie."

h. It is the best place for those who are most concerned with the best retirement and pension plans.

i. Failure-avoiders (as opposed to success-seekers) belong in the larger companies.

j. The giant firm is comfortable for people who find it psychologically important for them to be able to identify with an image of great power such as IBM, General Motors, United States Steel, Standard Oil, etc.

In addition to deciding on an industry and a company, and its size, you must also begin to fine tune the characteristics of the type of job in which you feel compatible or comfortable, and will offer to you the greatest opportunity. Perhaps some of the following guidelines may be of help:

1. You must decide the general field in which you want to

work, whether it be sales, accounting, personnel, manufacturing, etc.

2. Within a given field, sales for example, you should decide whether you want to sell a tangible, like a product, or whether you prefer to sell an intangible, like a service.

3. Would you be willing to travel?

4. What kind of clientele would you like to deal with?

5. Would you be willing to be transferred to another city?

You must decide the ground rules and restrictions under which you are willing to operate. It would not make a lot of sense to go with a large company like IBM on a permanent basis unless you were willing at some point to be transferred. (They used to say that IBM meant "*I Be Moving.*")

As you decide on your own personal ground rules and restrictions as what you will and will not do, you must recognize that with every restriction you are cutting down somewhat on your job potential. If you decide you will not move, will not travel extensively, etc., this is all right, but you should realize that in doing so you might be limiting yourself to fewer career possibilities.

One of the most important considerations is that you must determine the type of management with whom you can work effectively. Managements of companies, like individuals, have their own personalities. You should establish that you can "buy" the philosophy of the management of the company with whom you associate.

Some companies have management that is goal-oriented as opposed to being task-oriented. They are not conservative and are willing to take some chances. They are ambitious, free-wheeling type of people—highly leveraged, lean and hungry, etc.

Other types of companies might be more task-oriented. They are characterized by professional managers who are interested in protecting the status quo. They may be very conservative. They like things the way they are. They do not like a lot of change.

If you are a "swinger" yourself, you do not want to get with a very conservative management group. On the other hand, if you tend to be very conservative, you should not align yourself with a "swinging" type of management group.

The study of management types in various kinds of businesses is interesting and valuable. When you recognize the types of personalities in an organization, you can gear your strategy to the management personality of the organization.

Before you agree to accept a job, meet as many of the members of top management as possible in order that you can get some feel for this management personality. If the company you are considering is reluctant to have you meet other members of management, you should have some serious second thoughts. A prospective employer should be delighted to have you meet the members of the management team. If he feels otherwise, he may be hiding something. He may think so little of you as an individual that he does not want to take the time of management by having you talk to them; or it may be an indication that it is a "stuffy" type of traditional company that is *not* "low structured."

Low structured means the kind of company whose people rally around objectives. In this type of firm, the organizational chart tends to be very flat (not many levels), and communication is generally excellent; a lot of people seem to know what is going on in the company. Good relations usually exist between departments.

Before a company accepts you, in all probability they are going to check you out pretty thoroughly. They are going to check your references, your former employers, etc. The paradox is that your prospective employer is doing most of the checking; but you have the most to lose. If it does not work out, you will either get fired or you will quit and in the process have given up part of your most priceless commodity in business—the time during which you should be making real progress and becoming well established. It is a real tragedy to see a twenty-one-year-old man go with a company and, ten years later, realize that he has been completely incompatible with the company, and that his ten very valuable years were only slightly productive. Be very careful about making a commitment to go with an organization; check them out every way that you can. Talk to their bank, their suppliers, their clients, any source that can give you the best possible picture of the business before you go with them. Here is a personal example.

When I was twenty-one years old, I decided that I wanted to go into sales. My father, my mother and my grandfather had all been with Remington Rand. Naturally, I thought about Remington Rand when I considered going into sales. I called on the company, was interviewed and was offered a sales job in the tabulating machine division. I was fascinated by the punched card tabulating machines and I decided that there would certainly be a great future in this field.

In the process of checking out Remington Rand and the tabulating machine market I sought the advice of people for whom I had great respect. (I recommend this to you strongly. It is a very sincere form of flattery to the person whose advice you seek, no matter how important he may be. And you will receive a wealth of good advice. This is a habit I have maintained ever since I first started working. I do not always follow the advice, but I get objectivity.) I called on Dr. George Sparks, the president of what is now Georgia State University. I told him that I was considering taking a job with Remington Rand and asked what he would recommend. He indicated that since I was interested in tabulating machines I should also talk to IBM since they were the biggest in the field and had a good reputation. I had scarcely heard of IBM, this was 1952 and IBM's sales in those days were about $200 million (now they are over $8 billion). To make a long story short, I walked in off the street to IBM and asked for a job interview. After a rather lengthy process I went to work for IBM and it is a decision that I never regretted. Remington Rand was a fine organization but for my particular purpose IBM offered a better vehicle.

Before affiliating with any organization, check out their financial condition. This goes for large companies as well as for small companies. Large companies, at times, find themselves in financial difficulty. Companies like the Penn Central found themselves in serious trouble, as well as Boeing Aircraft, General Dynamics, Pan American World Airways, Lockheed, etc. Do not delude yourself into thinking that large size provides immunity from financial problems. In the case of small companies, I would look at their financial condition a little differently. I would want to make sure that the management is not running scared financially and fearing bankruptcy. In this case, you are sure to find irrational behavior—worse, you will be "riding a sick horse."

Many small companies are *not* in strong financial condition but the management and the other people in the organization are excited about what they are doing and are moving ahead with great enthusiasm. You can sense this feeling as you talk with the people in the organization. In this situation you have to ask yourself the following questions:

1. Can I get excited about this business and their plans? Am I willing to trade off a strong financial statement for an exciting concept?
2. Can I see myself as an integral part of making this company "go"?
3. Can I participate personally in the financial rewards if the company achieves its objectives?

In a smaller company you should determine what they started with and how far they have come. Marshall Mantler told me a story concerning a very large department store chain. The president asked some of his people why they were taking inventory. One of his people replied, "You want to know how much profit you have made, don't you?" The president took out a needle and a piece of thread and said, "This is what I started with. Everything else is profit."

Closely akin to the financial questions that I would ask about a small company are the questions I would ask finally about *any* company with which I was considering an affiliation. These are the things that I would want to know.

1. Where is this company now and where do they want to go?

2. What are their plans for getting there?
3. What authority and responsibilities will I have for participating in the achievement of the company objectives, and how will I be measured and compensated?
4. Will I be able to achieve my personal objectives and are they compatible with the objectives of the organization?
5. Do I really believe in what the company is trying to do? Can I internalize these beliefs—get them into my insides?
6. Has the company reached the stage of managerial maturity?

   Do they realize that the only real resource the company has is in the knowledge of its people and that its ability to grow and prosper will be a function of how well they can attract and retain good people in the organization?

   Do they realize that delegation means telling people what they are responsible for, not what to do? And, that it does not mean getting someone to assist in doing the manager's work, but rather giving responsibility and authority to the lowest level in the organization to which it can be properly given. The true meaning of management is getting work done through other people.

   Have they reached the point that they can no longer run the business like a big candy store in an intuitive manner in which they manage "by the seat of the pants"? Do they manage by objectives? (Even if they do not call it such, and perhaps never heard of Management By Objectives.)
7. Does the company have a reputation for integrity? A lasting business relationship involves a high degree of trust. If a company will cut corners with their clients, creditors, suppliers, etc., they will also cut corners with their employees.

> Nobody can really guarantee the future, The best we can do is size up the chances, calculate the risks involved, estimate our ability to deal with them, and then make our plans with confidence.
>
> —Henry Ford II

■ Don't Worry About Your Job Unless You Worry About Your Job

Worry is a thin stream of fear trickling through the mind. If encouraged, it cuts a channel into which all other thoughts are drained.
—Arthur Somers Roche

When you begin to worry about your job and its security, this is the time that you *need* to worry about it. It is an indication that you probably have misdirected your attention away from the *group* of which you are a part to that of the *individual job* which is your personal responsibility.

If you concern yourself with the objectives of your group, you will be able to keep your own job perspective relative to that of the group and your efforts will therefore be directed toward the group objectives.

When a person becomes truly worried about his individual job to the extent that he is no longer concerned with the group objectives, he is in trouble. His activities drift away from the group objectives and move toward protecting his job. As he attempts to insulate his particular job from the rest of the group in order to make his position more secure, he gets into deeper trouble, because his job can no longer be identified as being directed toward the group objectives.

As this process goes on, the person who previously was seeking success now suddenly becomes concerned with the avoidance of failure. He was previously highly motivated toward the attainment of the group objectives. He now develops a noticeable lack of confidence in himself and in his ability to do the job. The inevitable result is that he begins to play it safe, not wanting to "make waves."

A man might say to himself, "Why should I concern myself with the group? Everyone else is looking out for himself. Why should I try to be a hero and put the interest of the group ahead of my own interest?" The reason is quite simple and logical. When I say that you should put the interest of the group first, it is not "waving the flag." The reason is that you are measured by your contribution to the group of which you are a part. The organization's primary interest in your job has to do with how it relates to your group and to the organization as a whole. The only justification we have for working together in a group is that we can accomplish more by working together than we can by working as individuals. If this were not true, we would all make our own shoes, make our own clothes, raise our own food, etc.

> In business, as most of it is constituted to-day, a man becomes valuable only as he recognizes the relation of his work to that of all his associates. One worker more or less makes little difference to most big organizations, and that man may be replaced. It is the cumulative effort that counts.
>
> —W. Alton Jones

There was a small boy who had developed the habit of working first on one thing and then on another. He never seemed to finish anything. One day after a freshly fallen snow, his father said, "Son, let's go out and take a walk in the snow." When they got outside his father pointed to a tree at the far end of a big field and said to his son, "Let's see who can walk the straightest path to the tree." The boy very carefully kept placing one foot in front of the other until he arrived at the tree. At the same time, his father very casually walked in a normal manner until he arrived at the tree. When they both looked back at their tracks in the snow, the father's tracks were straight as an arrow, whereas the son's tracks zigzagged back and forth on the way to the tree. The father explained to the son that the reason his tracks were so straight was that as he walked he never took his eye off of his objective, which was the tree. He did not concern himself with the activity of walking straight and looking at his feet. By keeping his eye on his objective, he was able to keep his footsteps going in a straight path. His activity (walking) was more effective.

The boy on the other hand was so concerned with the job of putting one foot ahead of the other that he lost sight of the objective and created a zigzagged path to the tree.

So it is with the relationship between our own jobs and the objectives of our group. If we will concentrate on our objectives, the footsteps (our job) for getting there will take care of themselves in the most effective way.

Certainly everyone should have a *concern* (not worry) for his job, but it should be from the vantage point of the group. In the same manner, the whole organization has to view itself from the outside world, from the customer's point of view. This is where the results are.

It will be a sign of maturity in your thinking when you begin to realize that you have developed the attitude of looking at your own job in the context of the group and its objectives. Your attitude will become obvious to the others in the organization who share the same attitude and you will become a part of this group who are making something happen as opposed to the failure avoiders who are watching others make something happen.

The young man who would succeed must identify his interests with those of his employer and exercise the same diligence in matters entrusted to him as he would his own affairs.

—A. T. Mercier

■ Don't Let Your Daddy "Snow You"

This subject gets a little ticklish. I can talk rather freely inasmuch as my father died when I was eleven years old and due to his illness I had very little direct contact with him after I was in the first grade. As a result of losing my father at an early age, I developed an interest in observing the relationships between fathers and their sons. Because of my situation I was able to observe these relationships with some degree of objectivity. I said don't let your "daddy" snow you. Instead of daddy you might substitute big brother, uncle, boss, husband, wife, good friend or anyone else about whom you might develop myopia because of a close personal relationship. Of course you can learn from others. Learning, however, has nothing to do with hero worship, "blind faith," imitation, or the like.

Respect anyone you wish, but never lose sight of the fallibility of man. Although imitation is the most sincere form of flattery we cannot really "imitate" anyone. We can only be ourselves and try to improve by learning through observation of others. Every responsible father wishes to have a positive influence on his children; but having a positive influence does not translate to creating a carbon copy of yourself or trying to mold your offspring into all of the things that you always wanted to be but were not. The father who would do this is trying to relive his earlier life through his children. Trying to be someone else, even if it is to be a carbon copy of your father, is an enemy of success.

In rare instances you will hear of a son who "followed in his father's footsteps"; who was able to equal or surpass the accomplishments of the father. If by coincidence the son's aptitude and/or interest is the same as that of his father, then it is possible to excel. Many people in *IBM* felt that in many respects Thomas Watson, Jr. was a better businessman than his father, who had founded the company and had a great reputation as a businessman. As a matter of fact, Mr. Watson, Jr. said that what he had wanted to do was to be an airplane pilot, but succumbed to the natural influence and wound up with IBM. In the case of the great doctor who surpasses his doctor father, or the outstanding businessman who takes the father's business and makes it much bigger, (a la Howard Hughes, or Thomas J. Watson, Jr., or Sarnoff of R.C.A.), how many times they must have asked themselves "could I have done it on my own without the impetus provided by my father?"

If you face a decision as to whether or not to follow in your father's footsteps, I would do some soul searching as to whether later you will feel that you can live comfortably with this fact. If you are already following in your father's footsteps, I don't advocate slashing your wrists or quitting the family business. However, if I were in your position, I would vow to be my own man and recognize that I cannot be my father. I may dress like him, copy his mannerisms, try to speak with the same degree of authority, etc., but if I do, I hope that I would have the wisdom to recognize myself for what I would be, a cheap imitation. You must also pay the penalty of people comparing you to your father. Therefore, when you TRY to copy him, you are only adding fuel to the fire and you can bet that the comment is often made. "Look at the punk kid, trying to act like his old man."

Taking advice from someone like your father or anyone else to whom you feel quite close gets a little tricky. On one hand, because of the close relationship, we can expect a high degree of trust. On the other hand, because of the close relationship, it might be difficult to get an honest or unbiased answer; not dishonest in the sense of deception, but rather a case of a close relation having a tendency to perhaps tell you what you want to hear.

Try this little test. Go to your father, for example, and say "Hey Pop! I'm thinking of taking my life's savings and opening a tattoo shop. What do you think?" If he says, "Sounds like a great idea, son," then you've got a problem.

In 1966, I bought out my partner of several years in Management Services, Inc. My attorney, who was also a close friend, prepared the legal documents. After the papers had been prepared, and just prior to the closing, I went to another highly reputable law firm to get them to look over the terms of the agreement. This action was not precipitated by any lack of trust in my close friend and attorney, but rather to get a degree of objectivity from a source that was not as close to the situation. Listen to those to whom you are close, but always have a way of checking out their advice with someone who can give you more objectivity and will be quite willing to tell you that you are crazy as hell for wanting to open a tattoo shop.

I do not mean to imply, however, that people to whom you are close will give you bad advice. It can be some of the best advice that you can get.

One last word about the relationship of a father with his son. Often when a son follows in his father's footsteps, or attempts to imitate his father's style, it will deteriorate into a love/hate relationship as the wear and tear of constantly being compared to the father begins to take its toll.

The ideal arrangement is the type of relationship that my friend, George Wright, had with his father. George thinks his father was one of the greatest guys who ever lived and has been greatly influenced by his father in a very positive way and this is how it should be. George's father was a well-known minister. George is an outstanding salesman. Fortunately, George was able to love and respect his father in a noncompetitive type of environment. When father and son find themselves in a competitive environment, you sometimes see a reverse type of relationship where the disciple becomes greater than the master—or at least where the father suspects that the son is trying to outdo him. Then the father may come to resent his son. This is very often a problem that cannot be anticipated ahead of time, but develops very insidiously as the father and son begin to grow older and perhaps get a little more set in their ways. I have a friend in Atlanta who was in his father's business for years before resentment began to develop. The unpleasant result was that my friend resigned from the company and struck out on his own in a totally unrelated field. The story does have a happy ending. My friend became quite successful on his own and later became reconciled with his father on a father/son basis but never again as a business associate. I have another friend in Chicago by the name of Robert F. White, Jr. who now runs a business started by his father. His father now lives in Florida and leaves the running of the business to Bob. This family had the wisdom to work out their relationship on a businesslike basis, and the business is very successful.

Fathers and sons who are involved in business together would do well to bring in mutually-acceptable third parties such as lawyers, directors, or bankers and agree ahead of time that, with these third parties, they will negotiate "arm's length," businesslike arrangements that provide for: retirement, buy outs, compensation arrangements, authority, responsibility, etc. These points should be covered with more care than would be the case of a partnership in which the partners are NOT blood related. Contrary to the old saying, "blood is not thicker than water" when it comes to a business type of relationship.

It is unsophisticated, unbusinesslike and completely illogical to assume that because you are involved in business with someone close to you that it would be an insult or represent a lack of trust to want to establish the details of the relationship in black and white. I once created some ill feelings on the part of a relative of mine who wanted to borrow some money from me because I insisted that he sign a note to me for the amount involved. My attitude was quite simple. If this relative wanted me to give him the money, fine. No note would be necessary. If he wanted to truly borrow the money, I would not be a party to teaching him to be unbusinesslike by not requiring a note.

■ Who Is Being Interviewed?

A man should not say, "I would like to apply for a job." It is almost as disturbing to hear someone say, "I would like to be interviewed for a position with your company." Properly, a person should say, "I would like to arrange *an interview* for possible employment." You can tell much about a man's attitude toward his ability and his career by the way he expresses his desire to affiliate with your organization.

When a man says that he wants to apply for a job, this means that he wants to get on someone's payroll, anybody's payroll, and that he will do anything and he does not particularly care what it is.

When a man says that he wants to be interviewed for a position, this means that he wants the company to look him over and perhaps allow him to join the select group. He does not know what they might want him to do and he really is not very particular about what it will be. He just wants "in." An organization deludes itself if it feels flattered when a man is anxious to join blindly the organization with no questions asked. This man will never again look as good as he does the day before he comes to work for the organization. He is a highly skilled professional job seeker who will keep rapidly jumping from job to job without ever staying with one organization long enough to be measured based on his results.

Being subject to human nature, organizations naively assume that a man who comes to them making $12,000 per year should be offered $15,000 as an inducement to leave his present employer. He then comes with the organization for $15,000 per annum but leaves within six months to accept another job paying $18,000 without ever having been measured in the position paying $15,000. What happens to these people? Do they keep elevating themselves higher and higher until finally they have made a bundle and retire—without ever having worked?

How about the man who comes in with the attitude that he wants to arrange an interview for possible employment? This is the man with whom I want to talk. His attitude tells me that he may or may not want to work for our company. He wants to interview *us* just as much as we are interviewing *him*. And just as we are interested in checking his references, he wants to check ours. He may want to talk to the bank about us, or some of our large customers. If we hire this man we will feel fortunate that we have him instead of feeling that we did the man a favor by giving him a job. The company has a healthy attitude toward him. Here is a man who puts real value on his time and on his ability and would not have come with us if he did not think that he could put his ability and time to good use with our organization.

However, the MOST important reason for a prospective employee *to interview the organization* is that he has the most to lose if the relationship does not work out. This to me is another great paradox in business. The organization normally decides whether or not the man affiliates with the organization; yet the affiliation is more important to the man than to the organization. Logically, you would think that businesses would operate like college fraternities, "rushing" a prospective member who then chooses the organization with which he wants to affiliate.

The prospective employee has by far the most to lose. He is giving up part of his business life, his career, part of his formative years in business when he has to become well-established.

The organization has comparatively little to lose. All it can lose is some money and can always replace the man at its discretion.

■ Maybe the Boss Is the Guy in the White Hat

The younger and/or more inexperienced a man is in business, the more he tends to feel that he knows much more than does his manager. The manager is the "guy in the black hat." If you are in a position where you do not respect your manager, you should either get transferred to another manager or leave the organization. Before taking this radical step, however, you might first do some soul searching and try to view the situation with as much objectivity as possible. You might even consult with someone for whom you have respect, who knows all of the persons involved and could give you an unbiased viewpoint. It may very well be that after you have completed this exercise you will find that you have been in the wrong. Whether or not you are man enough to admit it is another matter.

Once again, I am speaking from experience. I have been there myself. When I was a young salesman with the IBM Corporation, my manager in Atlanta was Herbert E. Harris. I first feared this man. This fear had developed into dislike by the time I left IBM in 1957 at the age of twenty-six.

Several years later, after I had been in my own business for awhile, I began to start reflecting on what I had learned under Herb Harris and on the positive impact that he had on my business career. I found myself now doing the things I had criticized him for—to an even greater degree.

This began to prey on my conscience, because I was sure it had been obvious to Harris how I felt about him. I let this bother me from 1958 until about 1964 or 1965. Finally, to soothe my conscience, I wrote my former manager a letter. I told him how much his association had meant to me and how I realized that my dislike for him had been a manifestation of my immaturity in years and in business.

The situation reminded me of what Mark Twain had said to

the effect that when he was a very young man his father was a fool, but by the time he had grown up he discovered that his father had regained his senses.

My ex-manager responded to my letter and we began to stay in touch with each other. Today we are close friends, and he knows of the significant impact that he had on me as my manager. I feel it is appropriate that Herb Harris is one of the people to whom I have dedicated this book. My regret is that because of *my own* attitude at the time, I deprived myself of much more that I could have learned.

Managers, who get *their work* done through other people, are the most misunderstood group in business. It is difficult for the workers to appreciate the responsibilities and pressures that their managers have. All they can see is the "tip of the iceberg."

When you have a negative attitude toward your manager, you are depriving yourself of one of the very best ways to learn; that is to work under an effective manager. The apprentice system has been with us for centuries. This in itself is a pretty good endorsement for the method.

If you have a negative attitude toward your manager, it will be obvious to him unless he is very naive. Most managers did not get to be managers by being naive, but by being pretty savvy in their ability to "read" people.

If you work for me and I detect that you do not like me, my feelings will not be hurt. A manager cannot afford the luxury of running in a popularity contest with his people. However, I may equate your dislike for me with lack of respect. It is hard to respect a person whom you dislike. (There are exceptions— General Patton would perhaps be a good example. Many of the troops who hated him were the first in line behind him when it came time to do battle. This is respect.)

When your actions indicate that you *do not* respect me, I, in turn, *cannot* respect a person who would work for a manager whom *he* did not respect. There is a reaction for every action. If a man works for me without respecting me, I would consider him a coward for not leaving the business, and would say that his chances of succeeding would be very slim.

■ Find Yourself an Eagle

Great minds are like eagles, and build their nest in some lofty solitude.
—Arthur Schopenhauer

H. Ross Perot, the wealthy Texas businessman, was written up in *Fortune Magazine* in November, 1968. Perot has a large plaque on the wall of his office that reads: "Eagles Don't Flock, You Have To Find Them One At A Time." If I were a young man starting out in business, I would not settle for a company to work with until I had found an "eagle" under whom I could maximize my learning process. People from whom you can learn a great deal may be found even in the lower ranks of businesses.

Thomas J. Watson was a "gifted plagiarist"—a man who had the ability to absorb the good points of the people with whom he worked. John H. Patterson of the National Cash Register Company was one of Watson's eagles; and the evidence was seen all through the IBM organization after he left the National Cash Register Company.

You can make up for what you lack in experience to a large extent by working with people who do have the experience. If you let it, it will "rub off" on you.

As you begin to progress on the road to success you do not quit looking for eagles, you just look for them for a different purpose. How successful you are is usually a function of how good the people are whom you have been able to attract to work with you. Finding young eagles will enable you not only to implement your plans but they will keep you sharp by challenging you to try to stay ahead of them. Many men became successful by surrounding themselves with people who were smarter than they were. In fact, R. H. Grant said that "When you hire people who are smarter than you are, you prove you are smarter than they are." Often the strongest ability a man has is being able to put together the right kind of team. People with this kind of ability are not very conspicuous because, as they develop stronger teams, they themselves tend to fade into the wings. Robert Townsend in "Up The Organization"—quotes from Lao-tzu as follows:

> To lead the people, walk behind them.
> As for the best leaders, the people do not notice their existence.
> The next best, the people honor and praise.
> The next, the people fear; and the next, the people hate. . . .
> When the best leader's work is done the people say,
> "We did it ourselves!"

Millionaire Fletcher Jones was quoted in the December 3, 1965 issue of *Time Magazine* as having said: "To become a millionaire, you must get people behind you so that you can be multiplied."

Maybe you don't know any eagles. Perhaps you are in a job situation where you cannot very well move toward an eagle. How do you get the exposure?

Seek out people from whom you feel that you can learn and counsel with them. Ask them for their advice. Some of these people you may know, personally; others you may only know of through newspapers, reputation, etc. A successful person is flattered when someone is interested in his ideas and how he became successful. No matter how busy I am when I am asked questions about business success, etc., I will spend a great deal of time discussing these matters—even with people whom I might not ever have laid eyes on before. There are few things that successful people had rather talk about than success, their own or that of someone else.

As you become exposed to successful people you will begin to upgrade the type of people with whom you associate. This is not to imply that you will become a "snob." Quite naturally you will want to associate with other success-seekers; the search for success will become a strong bond between you. The old saying that "You can judge a man by the company he keeps" has a lot of wisdom in it.

We gain nothing by being with such as ourselves; we encourage each other in mediocrity. I am always longing to be with men more excellent than myself.

—Lamb

One reason so many successful people develop reputations as "loners" is that they prefer to associate with other successful people, and there are just not that many of them around. Another reason is that successful people become so consumed with what it is they are doing that they do become "loners" in many ways.

Many successful people prefer to spend time alone in creative solitude than to get with a "mind dulling" group of people whose only purpose for getting together is to mount a group offensive against boredom. A success-seeker does not know what it is to be bored, unless he is thrown into a boring situation—in which case he is usually able to escape.

Meeting successful people may be difficult because they often are not highly visible. Like eagles, they do not flock. You have to seek them out. Once you have found them, they are likely to be alone doing the thing that they like to do best, achieving success. But they may be very willing to stop and talk with you about how you can do the same.

A form of flattery that is not particularly appealing to most successful people is to TELL them that they did something well. They usually know it, and that is sufficient unto itself. In my time, I have consummated some rather major (to me) business transactions after overcoming some overwhelming odds against me. When I have done this, it has been obvious to me and to the people with whom I am dealing. In these instances, it means practically nothing to me for someone to tell me that I did a good job. I know I did a good job. BUT, if a man asks me how I managed to overcome the odds and accomplish what I did, he has me wrapped around his little finger.

If I wanted to become a tramp, I would seek information and advice from the most successful tramp I could find. If I wanted to become a failure I would seek advice from men who have never succeeded. If I wanted to succeed in all things, I would look around me for those who are succeeding, and do as they have done.

—Joseph Marshall Wade

■ How Well Do You Throw the Spear?

Make the most of yourself, for that is all there is to you.

—Emerson

It is estimated that there are more than 200,000 millionaires in the United States today as opposed to approximately 67,000 in 1962. Some people say that it is easier to become successful now than it used to be. This is what they say when they are explaining the success of *others*. However, when they are trying to justify their *own* lack of success they take just the opposite viewpoint. They say it is much more *difficult* to become successful today than it used to be. This line of reasoning is irrelevant. What difference does it make whether it is easier or more difficult to be successful now than it used to be? You cannot live in the past. You can live only today and on into the future, so why concern yourself with the previous climate for success. It is too late to be successful in the past.

For any given period of time you want to pick, going all the way back to the days our ancestors were swinging in the trees or throwing spears to obtain food, some guys were always able to throw the spear better than others. "The cream always rises to the top." This is why you should concern yourself with those now in the game, not your ancestors. It is a little like arguing about whether Joe Louis could have defeated Jack Dempsey, or if current baseball world champions could have defeated the New York Yankees of the thirties.

The point is that "now" is where the action is, so quit digging into the past looking for a "cop-out."

Successful men do the best they can with conditions as they find them and seldom wait for a better turn.

—William Feather

■ Let's Get Divorced—Business Wise

I never have told anyone in my organization that he was "fired." To "fire" a man has the connotation of "drumming him out of the corps," or driving him out of the city walls like some kind of a leper. It has all of the implications of disgrace, and it really should not be this way. When you "terminate" a relationship with someone in the organization, it is not pleasant. However, a termination in business should be logical and rational. It should not be a bitter process like divorce.

The important thing that is often overlooked when a termination takes place is that it is not only a disappointment for the employee, it is also a disappointment for the organization. It usually represents a substantial financial loss, (waste) of the money that was spent in the training of the man, in addition to losses that he probably caused by not doing a satisfactory job. Also, it will cost money to replace the man. However, perhaps the biggest cost is unknown; it is the cost of having the wrong man in the wrong position.

Logically, the man being terminated should feel apologetic for the fact that the company found it necessary to terminate him. However, this is not the way that it is in the real world. Terminated employees are often bitter and highly resentful toward the company. If this same employee, instead of being terminated by the company, decided that he would terminate the relationship with the company and quit, he would do so without any apologetic feelings or sense of obligation toward the company. Indeed, the employee who quits may even be given a luncheon by his fellow employees and showered with gifts.

Organizations do not hire a person with the idea of getting the best out of him and then getting rid of him. Hiring a new employee is an investment which normally takes a considerable amount of time before it begins to pay off. The worst possible solution to a personnel problem is termination. You already have the employee. You have invested time and money in him. He probably has developed a considerable amount of expertise that will go out of the door when he leaves. Termination has negative implications if the other employees have any idea that the person was not dealt with fairly. (You can bet that they have heard his side of the story from him.)

There is also a psychological problem here. If you are considering the termination of an employee, subconsciously you may begin to look for the negative qualities that will support your possible decision to terminate him. At the same time, there may be other candidates outside of the company whom you are considering. The situation then boils down to this. On one hand you are focusing on the negative traits of the existing employee and at the same time you are looking at the positive traits of his potential replacement. A new employee will never look as good to you again as he does the day before he comes to work in your organization. All that you can see is the good in the potential replacement. He looks like a knight in shining armor.

Having to terminate an employee is often not the real problem; it is only a symptom of the problem. The problem was hiring the man in the first place. Therefore, we should consider the hiring process briefly. If we spent more time concerning ourselves with the qualifications of people before they came into the organization, we could spend a lot less time worrying about what to do with the "misfit" who is already in the organization.

One simple device that has improved our batting average in hiring new people is to have at least three people in the organization interview the prospective employee. If he is being considered for a real key position, we might also have him interviewed by one of our directors or some other outside source who is close to our organization.

In spite of all the controversy over testing as an effective tool in hiring, I do believe in tests as a negative indicator. Tests more often will uncover "the chinks in a man's armor" than they will uncover his real strengths. Although tests can point out the strengths of a man, his strengths are usually more easily detectable during the interview when we have an opportunity to ask "in depth" questions.

In interviewing a prospective employee, there are two key

questions that I always ask. I first ask: "What do you think that your real strengths are?" The prospective employee usually will not come up with any real surprises because he will probably tell you of the strengths that you have already detected, or the strengths that he wants you to think that he has. Now for the "biggie." I then ask the prospective employee: "What do you think your *weaknesses* are in order of importance?" If he says that he has no weaknesses, I conclude the interview as soon as possible and thank him for his time. (We do not have any openings for people who walk on water.) Usually the man will hesitate before answering; and if he hesitates for too long or tells me that he has never thought about it before, this also tells me a lot about the man. This in itself is a weakness—the fact that he has not practiced enough introspection to know what his "short suits" are. It is unlikely that when the man does tell you his weaknesses that he will make them up (as he might do in the case of his strengths). He will probably be quite honest about the weaknesses that he will mention—although it is unlikely that he will give them to you in the right sequence of importance. It is also likely that he will not tell you about his biggest weakness, (being an alcoholic, for example), but at least you are beginning to develop a picture of the man that was not obvious before.

It is important that you check a man's references. His personal references usually do not mean much. I have yet to check a personal reference that was unfavorable. (Would you give anyone for a reference who would say that you are a bum?) When checking the man's former employers, ask them the same questions about the strengths and the weaknesses of the man. Then compare what they tell you against what the man has told you regarding his strengths and weaknesses. This is almost always a very interesting exercise.

I do not mean to oversimplify. The hiring process is complex, and at best is not very exacting, but these simple procedures have been highly effective for me.

Whenever anyone indicates to me that they are faced with the unpleasant responsibility of having to terminate an employee and are filled with dread at the anticipation, I invariably tell them to read page 89 of the *Effective Executive* by Peter Drucker. It is the finest summary of the true situation that I have ever seen. I do not believe that in the years since I first read "page 89," I have ever terminated an employee without rereading the following passage just prior to having terminated him:

> It is the duty of the executive to remove . . . anyone . . . who consistently fails to perform with high distinction. To let such a man stay on corrupts the others. It is grossly unfair to the whole organization. It is grossly unfair to his subordinates who are deprived by their superior's inadequacy of opportunities for achievement and recognition. Above all, it is senseless cruelty to the man himself. He knows that he is inadequate whether he admits it to himself or not. Indeed, I have never seen anyone in a job for which he was inadequate who was not slowly being destroyed by the pressure and the strains and who did not secretly pray for deliverance.

Keeping a man who should be terminated jeopardizes the jobs of the other employees to the degree that the man has a negative impact on the total organization. If this person is in a managerial position, the problem is even more serious. The effectiveness of the people who report to this manager is to a large degree a result of the effectiveness of the manager. To render his subordinates less effective by keeping the manager in the organization is immoral.

To keep a man on after the time that he should be terminated really is "senseless cruelty" to the man himself. You are putting off the inevitable by not terminating him, and everyday that you keep him is just one less day he will have to make a place for himself elsewhere. To the organization this man can cost money. To the man himself, you are taking part of his life, his business life. An organization has a moral obligation to a man not to take any more of his business life than is absolutely necessary once it has been established that he should be terminated.

Some managers can not face up to the realization that they should terminate one of their people. This can be a serious deficiency. When we first put a person in a managerial position, I always ask if he has ever had to terminate anyone, and if not, would he have any reservations about doing so? We also make it clear that one of the most serious mistakes that he could make as a manager would be to keep a man on even one day after the man should have been terminated.

The most unfortunate situation in this regard is where the job has outgrown the man. Fortunately, in a growing company, there are opportunities for lateral movements of people into other areas where they can be effective. An organization has an obligation to go to great lengths to work out a satisfactory arrangement with an employee whose responsibilities have outgrown him. The employee has been an asset to the company or he would have been terminated before. Furthermore, there can be a far-reaching impact on morale if others feel that if they do not keep up with the pace of the company they will be terminated. And there is another point in favor of lateral movement. People go through a rather erratic pattern of growth and development. At times it will appear that a man is "topping out." Later he seems to find himself, and again progresses in his work. Too rapid termination deprives the company of the benefit of this renewed progress.

How about the employee? What should his attitude be when he finds himself terminated? Will it destroy him or make him stronger for the experience? If it is of any comfort, a great many successful people were fired at one time or another, including Thomas J. Watson and J. C. Penney (who didn't do too badly in business). Watson, who was fired at the age of forty and then built the IBM organization, should be a good example for anyone who thinks that getting fired is the end of the world. Let's assume that a man has done what he considers to be his best in an organization. Mr. Watson obviously did before he was fired as sales manager by the National Cash Register Company. The obvious conclusion that a person should come to is that he was terminated because his objectives and those of the organization were not compatible. It is not because he was a low form of animal life and a failure as a human being. If your objectives and those of the organization are not compatible and somebody has to go, obviously the rest of the organization cannot go, (unless you happen to own the store in which case the golden rule becomes: "Those who have the gold make the rules.").

Someone once said that "you cannot get a second chance at a first impression." I would paraphrase that by saying that "you cannot get a second chance at a *last* impression." I have often learned more about a person during the last fifteen minutes that he was with our company than during all of the rest of the time that he had been with us. The reason is that in the last fifteen minutes people tend to show their true colors. Before you may have seen only a facade.

If you are ever terminated, go out in a blaze of glory. Work as hard the last day as you would the first day on the job. No matter how unfairly you might feel that you were dealt with, you can only hurt yourself by "unloading" your stored-up antagonisms as you leave the business. Your past is like a chain with no unbroken links. Although you might derive a lot of satisfaction by giving your boss hell on your last day with the organization, you will probably live to pay dearly for that satisfaction. You should assume a positive attitude and acknowledge that you are better off being terminated than to be left in a position where the firm has mentally terminated you but had left you on the payroll. This only wastes precious time in which you could become established with another organization with whom you could be more compatible.

To retain ill feelings toward an organization after you have left can only work on you like a disease. And it is of no use. While you are walking around hating your old boss or the company, they will have probably forgotten your name. Hate is a "boomerang" in business. You are the one who stands to get hurt.

When you leave with obvious good will toward the company, and you make known your feelings, they will respect you for it; and they will probably go to great lengths to help you in any way that they can in the future, including the providing of a good reference for anyone who inquires.

It is hard for me to understand how anyone can work for a company for a long time; earn the opportunity to get a good reference; secure the good will of the former employer; and then "blow it" fifteen minutes before they leave the company for the last time.

I am reminded of the employee who was fired and wrote his former boss expressing his sentiments. His former boss wrote back thanking the employee for his sentiments, but observing, "I appreciated your sentiments very much, but your spelling was atrocious. You spelled lousy with a *z* and bastard with two *s*'s." This, unfortunately, is the way too many people choose to leave an organization.

Decisions—
Big and Little

The road to success is not to be run upon by seven-leagued boots. Step by step, little by little, bit by bit—that is the way to wealth, that is the way to wisdom, that is the way to glory.

—Charles Buxton

RECENTLY my six-year-old daughter became very frustrated in making a decision as to which of two beds she should choose for her room. Decision-making is relative, whether it is a six year old choosing a bed, a teen-ager selecting a new dress, a college student selecting a curriculum or a big business tycoon deciding to buy a building. The tycoon probably decides to buy the building with less anxiety than my six-year-old chooses a bed, because he is better equipped to make the decision and is probably used to making decisions of this magnitude. In the case of the tycoon, it might even have been a relatively minor decision.

Actions that we take and decisions that we make are only as large or as small as we see them. When you start out, you may be awed by the magnitude of decisions that you observe and read about. The way to do the big is to do the little. Big decisions and big achievements usually come about through an evolutionary process. As you grow in your work, the size of your decisions and accomplishments grows proportionately, with the result that at any given stage in your development you will probably be equal to the task at hand. *Big decisions often are not so much big decisions as they are the logical conclusion of having made a number of small decisions.* This was the case when our company came to the logical conclusion that we should purchase a computer system for $560,000 in 1969. It was actually less of a *decision* than the decision that we made in 1961 to purchase a piece of IBM equipment for $22,000, because there was actually less risk involved from the standpoint of being able to justify the expenditure in the case of the larger computer system.

It is the evolutionary nature of our development that makes it difficult for us to observe this growth in ourselves. We are too close to the situation to be aware of it. (They say that fish are the last to discover the water.) More often other people see this development in you before you realize it yourself.

However, there are times when we are called on to achieve that which appears to be more of a challenge than we are equipped to handle, but because we have to do it, we do it. It is during these periods that we are most aware of our capacity to achieve. There are times when we are able to accomplish far beyond that which we thought we could, only to have a specific project fail. In situations like this we feel we have climbed Mount Everest, to no avail, without anyone having known about it. This, however, is a shortsighted and negative viewpoint. What is important, even when a project of great magnitude fails, is that *we know* what we were able to do and we should emerge with the positive attitude that we are stronger and wiser for having had the experience.

> Undertake something that is difficult; it will do you good. Unless you try to do something beyond what you have already mastered, you will never grow.
>
> —Ronald E. Osborn

There is a mythical "wheeler dealer" type of business executive whose every decision is of monumental importance. He has no time for details. He can make snap decisions on very important matters with only a smattering of information. This makes for good entertainment in movies and books like *Cash McCall* and *The Executive Suite*. But the real world is not this way. In fact it is just the opposite. Big decisions are usually not big decisions at all, but the automatic by-product of a lot of little decisions, made slowly and deliberately and often involving quite a bit of detail.

If you are constantly faced with big decisions on a crisis basis without knowing the details, you are mismanaging your business. The hare is faster at times but inconsistent and in the long run, betting on the tortoise is probably good business. In the commodity market, the "fast buck" boys who come in to make a big killing in the market have a way of disappearing from the scene whereas most of the plodders are still playing the game.

> Success is the sum of detail. It might perhaps be pleasing to imagine oneself beyond detail and engaged only in great things, but as I have often observed, if one attends only to great things and lets the little things pass, the great things become little; that is, the business shrinks.
> —Harvey S. Firestone

■ If You Want to Launch Big Ships You Have to Go to Deep Water

Conrad Hilton, in his book *Be My Guest*, points out that he was a native of San Antonio, New Mexico. His mother indicated to him that if he wanted to launch big ships he would have to go to where the water is deep. This does not necessarily mean physically moving to a different location or to a bigger town. Many people decide to go to big cities because they believe there is more opportunity there. True, there is a lot of opportunity but there are also a lot of people there competing for the opportunity. Unfortunately, many people in smaller communities cannot see the woods for the trees. They overlook the greatest opportunities right under their noses. I have a good friend by the name of J. Walter Moore who lives in the very small town of Hayesville, North Carolina. Hayesville is a beautiful town situated on a large lake, surrounded by mountains. Most of the people who grew up with J. Walter left the area to seek their fortunes elsewhere. J. Walter has never left the area and has been a success, financially and otherwise. He is a "trader" by nature and has been in a variety of businesses, always walking away with more than he came in with. J. Walter does everyday what many people "beat their brains out" to do when they retire at sixty-five.

Russell Conwell's famous *Acres of Diamonds* is a story about a farmer who sold his farm and all of his worldly goods in order to get enough money to travel and to discover diamonds. After years of searching and discouragement, the farmer committed suicide, a failure. Years later while plowing the fields, the man who had purchased the farm noticed that his plow had struck an object and that it had a brilliant glow. You can guess the rest. The man had discovered diamonds on the very spot where the previous farmer had lived. The farm turned out to be one of the largest deposits of diamonds in the world.

The example is clear. Often we are literally sitting on acres of diamonds but go elsewhere in our quest for a fortune. In reading about various business successes, it is surprising to see how often someone from outside an industry will come up with the really great ideas for that industry. This was true with Holiday Inn. The man who started Holiday Inn was in the construction business and had gotten "fed up" while on vacation with all of the "crummy" hotels with no restaurants, charging extra for children, tips, etc. He decided that he would start a chain of motels where people would know ahead of time what they could expect in the way of quality and service. It took a man associated with a company that made milk shake machines to discover the gold mine in a small hamburger stand by the name of McDonald's. Fried chicken had been with us for a long time, but Colonel Sanders put it all together.

It happens with countries also. The United States discovered the tiny transistor, but it took the Japanese to see the potential it had for making small inexpensive radios and other miniaturized products. So when you decide to launch your big ships, before you decide to go to another country, city, company, etc., look around and make sure you are not already sitting in the middle of a deep channel.

■ Luck Is a "Cop-out"

> It will generally be found that men who are constantly lamenting their ill luck are only reaping the consequences of their own neglect, mismanagement, and improvidence, or want of application.
>
> —S. Smiles

You hear businessmen talk a lot about "luck" in business. I'll be honest. This irritates me.

I have an aunt who lives in North Carolina who commented to me, "Aren't you lucky that you went into the kind of business that you did?" My reply was, "Not really. I can think of several types of businesses in which I could have probably done better." Her comment had not bothered me. My aunt knows very little about business and did not know any better. But when a businessman talks about luck it's something else again. Anyone who is involved in business has to virtually *ignore luck*. This is not to deny the existence of luck, good or bad. The reason you should *ignore* luck is that there is nothing you can do about pure luck any more than you can do anything about your age, your relatives, or baldness.

In his book, *How To Be A Successful Executive*, John Paul Getty, probably the richest man on earth was quoted as saying:

> Reaching the upper rungs of the ladder of corporate success is hardly a matter of luck. Few, if any, of our modern-era business executives are born. Virtually all of them are made, in the sense that they are produced by various processes of education, training, and experience.

Unfortunately, in an attempt to be modest, many people shrug off an outstanding accomplishment by saying, "I was just lucky, I guess."

My hard-driving, positive thinking, good friend, Dr. David J. Schwartz has no time for luck, one way or the other. In his great book *The Magic of Thinking Big*, Dave has the following to say about luck:

> Take a second look at what appears to be someone's "good luck." You'll find not luck, but preparation, planning, and success-producing thinking preceded his good fortune. Take a second look at what appears to be someone's bad luck. Look, and you'll discover certain specific reasons.

Elsewhere this book emphasizes the importance of front end effort—the concept that if you do more than what you are paid for, you ultimately will be paid for more than you do. It is all too easy for many people to attribute the results of others' success to luck when actually it is a result of hard work, drive, and goal-directed action.

What often appears to be good luck is only good judgement. A lot of "bad luck" is just bad judgement.

Mike Todd once said that "he worked hard at being lucky." Mr. Todd made the discovery made by many successful men— that the harder he worked, the luckier he got.

Conrad Hilton had the following to say about luck:

> I do believe in luck. But the kind I believe in has to do with people, and being in the right place at the right time, and receptive to new ideas.
>
> All my life long I have only been as good as my associates, and in them have found my good luck, my fortune.

Mr. Hilton looks upon some of his *failures* as good luck. He feels that he was "lucky" in that every time things started going well and he became complacent, something or someone always brought him back to reality again. Most people would call this bad luck. It was *good* for Conrad Hilton.

We should not acknowledge the presence of luck, *or any other factor over which we have no real control*, as being an impediment on our road to success. You *must* concern yourself with the elements over which you do have control.

There isn't any luck that enters into anything, unless it's poker or shooting dice, maybe. There is no luck to merchandising. There is no luck in going out and working from early in the morning to long after dinner. That is not luck, it's work.

—Fred W. Fitch

■ Sleep on It!

When, against one's will, one is high pressured into making a hurried decision, the best answer is always "no," because "no" is more easily changed to "yes," than "yes" is changed to "no."

—Charles E. Nielson

Almost without exception, any time that I have ever made a decision of any importance hastily when it was not imperative that I do so, I have learned to regret it. Whenever I can "sleep on it" overnight I find that I am more likely to make a good decision. Before you accuse me of procrastination, let me defend myself. When I was heavily speculating in the commodity market, decisions often had to be made in seconds. When people stand around trying to make up their minds what to do, the market decides for them. I have a history of acting as fast as I *need* to act when it comes to making decisions. However, I become very sensitive when I feel that I am being pressured into acting prematurely. Some automobile and real estate salesmen are masters of creating a sense of urgency about having to make an immediate decision before the deal slips by.

Considering a problem overnight gives you the opportunity to take the problem out of the office, away from the field of battle, where you can quietly and rationally consider the alternatives. You may agonize over a difficult problem and look at several seemingly equal alternatives during the day; then think some more about the problem that night. When you wake up the next morning, refreshed and clearheaded, the answer often becomes obvious whereas the night before you were uncertain.

President Nixon said, "When the action is hot, keep the rhetoric cool." Delaying a decision until stress and emotions can cool down tends to improve objectivity. Tempers flare up in business as they do in other places. When tempers are hot, this is not the time to be making decisions.

Once your business associates become accustomed to your style of making decisions, it will help them eliminate some of their own crises. They will know that you will not be forced into a hasty decision and they will develop the habit of approaching their problems more rationally in order that a hasty on-the-spot decision will not be necessary when you are involved.

People who always appear to be in a crisis usually create the crises for themselves. In many instances it is almost a form of self-torture. They seem to delight in creating a horrible situation with great pressure requiring snap decisions. The snap decisions in turn compound the problem in that they often are the wrong decisions.

Unfortunately we have developed a myth about executives making fast decisions to the extent that "thinking it over" is often considered a sign of weakness. Movies and novels about business have not helped matters any, with executives making decisions right and left in machine gun fashion without a moment's hesitation.

When you are told that you must make a decision immediately or miss out on a hot business opportunity, your normal reply should be "If I have to make a decision right now the answer will have to be no." The person who has been in such a hurry for a decision suddenly finds that the next day will be soon enough. There is a by-product advantage of telling someone that you want to think about a proposition overnight. They often construe this as a lack of enthusiasm on your part toward their idea and they may make you a better deal right on the spot.

Because of a lack of self-confidence, many people feel that it is a sign of weakness on their part if they are not able to make immediate decisions. You must eliminate this type of thinking from your mind. I do not lack for self-confidence, but common sense tells me that anyone who has been wrong as many times as I have should take an adequate amount of time to weigh all of the available facts before making a decision. You seldom have all of the facts about any decision, and I do not advocate trying to get them all. This would be an exercise in futility. But you can improve the slight edge that one man may have over another by being more deliberate in your decision-making process.

■ Advice or Agreement

It is expedient to have an acquaintance with those who have looked into the world; who know men, understand business, and can give you good intelligence and good advice when they are wanted.

—B. Horne

Often when people ask you for advice, they really don't want your advice. What they want you to do is to agree with them in order that they can fortify their decision to do a certain thing. If you are honest with yourself, you will recall plenty of times when you have asked for the advice of people when what you really wanted was for them to agree with you. The easiest way for you to find this agreement is to ask someone who works for you or a softhearted friend or a member of the family who will be only too happy to agree with you about almost anything.

If you need to go through this exercise occasionally to build up your confidence, fine. But, let's recognize it for what it is. It is not advice, it is agreement. If you really want to get advice from people, (incidentally, asking for advice is one of the best ways to win people over) it takes skill. In fact, getting advice is really an art. You must be able to ask a person for advice in such a way that you do not "telegraph" your opinion, or otherwise he will probably just tell you what he thinks you want to hear. This is human nature. Why jeopardize a friendship or a working relationship by telling a man something he doesn't want to hear when you know he has already made up his mind about what he is going to do?

Whenever I am asked for advice by someone, and it is obvious to me before I give the advice what his position is, I ask "Do you want me to tell you what I think, or do you want me to tell you what you want to hear?" In most instances, it is difficult to tell someone something that is obviously contrary to the way he thinks.

Some people want to make sure of getting the kind of advice (agreement) they are looking for. So they start with "Would you agree with me that I ought to do so-and-so"; or "I think we ought to take this specific action. What do you think?" What the hell are you supposed to say when you are asked for advice on this basis?

There are too few people around who will really give you sound advice. So what do we do? We go to them and ask them for advice, and they don't tell us what we want to hear, so we react negatively. This is the last time we get advice from this source. Henceforth, it will be only agreement. If he is still speaking to you.

There is an old saying that "advice is worth what you pay for it." This simply is not true. There is an abundance of worthwhile, good advice around that is free, or virtually free, for the asking. This book is an attempt to offer what I consider to be good advice. If you are reading a borrowed copy, it is costing you only your time. There are few things more flattering to people than to be asked for advice. It has an almost magical effect. It tears down all kinds of barriers between people, within the family, in business, between a man and his manager or his co-workers, in selling situations between a salesman and the prospect, etc. In some instances, it makes good sense to ask for advice when you really do not want the advice, just as a means of establishing a good relationship. Here again, however, recognize it for what it is.

Getting advice does not necessarily lead to following the advice. Only you can make this decision after you have weighed the logic of the advice with your own thinking. Receiving advice, however, gives you objectivity that you cannot possibly get within yourself.

You have to weigh the LOGIC of the advice. You often have to look beyond the conviction of the person from whom you get the advice, to the logic of what he has said. It is true that more believers are made by the depth of a man's conviction than by the height of his logic. As a result, therefore, a man may be absolutely wrong in his thinking, but because of the depth of his conviction he can color the logic of the matter.

This is why you should write the problem down on paper with all of the alternate solutions. This tends to take a lot of the emotion out of the picture and allows you to view your decision in a more detached manner. If you have ever been in New York City and have asked a cab driver for his advice on *any* subject, with all of the conviction in the world he will give you advice even if he hasn't the slightest idea of what he is talking about. The first couple of times you encounter a New York cab driver you get the feeling that perhaps he should be running the government or negotiating with the Red Chinese instead of driving the cab. After several more cab rides, amazingly enough you realize that all of the cab drivers are equally as smart.

If I were to name the real key reasons for any degree of success that I have enjoyed, one would have to be that I have always sought out and listened to advice. For example, I have been very active in my trade association and although I have given freely of any advice I had to others, at the same time I have been careful to absorb as much advice as I could gather. Then I have sifted out those parts which seemed the most logical. It has been time and money well spent for me to travel to other cities or to make long distance calls to seek out the advice of others. Why keep reinventing the wheel? Why not gather up the experience of others and conserve your energies for more creative matters?

> Associate with men of judgement, for judgement is found in conversation, and we make another man's judgement ours by frequenting his company.
>
> —Fuller

7

Managing—
Yourself and Others

The best executive is the one who has sense enough to pick good men to do what he wants done, and self-restraint enough to keep from meddling with them while they do it.

—Theodore Roosevelt

LONG BEFORE the birth of Jesus Christ, the Harvard Business School, and the American Management Association, there were good and bad managers. Some were men who intuitively practiced professional management. Others did not start off by being good managers, but learned to manage well. Moses is an excellent example of someone who *learned* to be a good manager.

The next day Moses took his seat to settle disputes among the people, and they were standing round him from morning till evening. When Jethro, the father-in-law of Moses, saw all that he was doing for the people, he said "what are you doing for all these people? Why do you sit alone with all of them standing round you from morning till evening?" "The people come to me," Moses answered, "to seek God's guidance. Whenever there is a dispute among men, they come to me, and I decide between man and man. I declare the statutes and laws of God." But his father-in-law said to Moses, "This is not the best way to do it. You will only wear yourself out and wear out all the people who are here. The task is too heavy for you; you cannot do it by yourself. Now listen to me: take my advice, and God be with you. It is for you to be the people's representative before God, and bring their disputes to him. You must instruct them in the statutes and laws, and teach them how they must behave and what they must do. But you must yourself search for capable, God-fearing men among all the people, honest and incorruptible men, and appoint them over the people as officers over units of a thousand, of a hundred, of fifty or of ten. They shall sit as a permanent court for the people; they must refer difficult cases to you but decide simple cases themselves. In this way your burden will be lightened, and they will share it with you. If you do this, God will give you strength and you will be able to go on. And, moreover, this whole people will here and now regain peace and harmony." Moses listened to his father-in-law and did all he had suggested. He chose capable men from all Israel and appointed them leaders of the people, officers over units of a thousand, of a hundred, of fifty or of ten. They sat as a permanent court, bringing the difficult cases to Moses, but deciding simple cases themselves.

—Exodus 18:13–26

Jethro was a good manager intuitively. He understood that management is getting things done *through other people*. Moses was an able student; he learned Management By Objectives from his father-in-law.

Almost anyone with any degree of intelligence CAN learn to be a manager of people, BUT there are many people who should never become managers simply because they can be of more value to themselves and their organizations by being "doers." Unfortunately, we have built up the image of the manager to the extent that many people feel they must aspire to be a manager; otherwise they will be classed as unambitious. This is not as it should be. If a man aspires to be a manager *and* has the aptitude, fine. But people should not be made managers just because they have established good records as *doers*.

Nevertheless, people are generally promoted into management because they have distinguished themselves as doers. In effect the company says, "since you have done a good job doing one thing, we are going to promote you into a position where you will be doing something entirely different." Managing is a discipline unto itself. Although I take serious issue with *The Peter Principle*, I do agree that *at times* people are promoted to their level of inefficiency, at which point they are no longer promotable and are therefore left in a position of inefficiency. The tragedy is that an excellent mechanic might make a lousy shop foreman, and often the worst sales manager you could appoint would be your star salesman. The result is that you have lost a good doer and gained a lousy manager.

It is extremely difficult and requires a great amount of self-discipline to shift gears from being a doer to being a manager. The difficulty of making this transition is compounded by the average person's refusal to study management principles when he finds himself thrust into this new environment. There are excellent books on the subject. Peter Drucker's *The Effective Executive* should be read by everyone in business and studied carefully by anyone in management or who aspires to be in management. In this book, Drucker points out very well the essence of the point:

> Executives are forced to keep on "operating" unless they take positive actions to change the reality in which they live and work. Executives graduate, as a rule, out of functional work and operations, and cannot slough off the habits of a lifetime when they get into general management. . . . Unless he changes it by deliberate action, the flow of events will determine what he is concerned with and what he does. If the executive lets the flow of events determine what he does, what he works on, and what he takes seriously, he will fritter himself away "operating."

This was the problem that Moses was having. He was frittering himself away operating until his father-in-law taught him some management fundamentals. It's still the same old circus. We just have a new set of clowns.

■ Delegation, Abdication and Servitude

> No matter how much work a man can do, no matter how engaging his personality may be, he will not advance far in business if he cannot work through others.
>
> —John Craig

An effective delegator walks the razor's edge between abdication on one hand and servitude on the other. The concept of delegation is widely misunderstood, and what is often referred to as delegation is not delegation at all. It is either abdication or servitude.

Let's define *abdication* as the complete relinquishing of responsibility, authority and accountability. *Servitude* is at the other end of the spectrum. We will define servitude as the lack of freedom to determine one's course of action.

Delegation is the reliance on the ability of someone to be responsible and accountable for that which was entrusted to him, and for which sufficient authority has been given.

It is popular in business for men to say that you can delegate authority but not responsibility. You *can* delegate authority *and* responsibility *but* you must maintain control. The person to whom you delegate is accountable to you. You, in turn, cannot relinquish your accountability to whomever delegated to you. Accountability in my mind is an inseparable part of responsibility.

If my manager delegates responsibility to me and I, in turn, delegate all or part of this responsibility to someone who reports to me, this does not "get me off the hook" with my manager. *I* am accountable to my manager, not the person to whom I delegated the responsibility. My manager is looking to me for the accountability and that is as it should be. This seems obvious, but many people miss it. Too often when I have delegated a responsibility to a manager, and asked him later why the objective was not accomplished, I get the answer that he turned it over to someone else and they just did not get it done. To compound the felony, the manager feels he has discharged his accountability when he, in turn, has delegated the responsibility to one of his people.

Abdication, then, is when we relinquish responsibility and authority, exercise no control and do not hold anyone accountable for the responsibility.

Servitude, as we have said, means the lack of freedom to determine one's own course of action. This occurs when someone thinks that delegation means telling someone *what to do* instead of telling him *what it is that he is responsible for*. When a manager is guilty of this, he reduces his people to the level of coolies, but usually not for long. If these coolies happen to be success-seekers they will soon leave the organization. I impose *servitude* when I asked you to help me do *my* work. I *delegate* when I give you a part of my responsibility. Peter Drucker expressed the true concept of delegation when he stated:

> As usually presented, delegation makes little sense. If it means that somebody else ought to do part of "my work," it is wrong. One is paid for doing one's own work . . . an enormous amount of the work being done by executives is work that can easily be done by others, and therefore should be done by others. "Delegation" as the term is customarily used, is a misunderstanding—is indeed misdirection. But getting rid of anything that can be done by somebody else so that one does not have to delegate but can really get to one's own work—that is a major improvement in effectiveness.

If you are a manager, the extent to which you will continue to grow in your organization can very well be a direct result of your ability to delegate in the true sense of the word. This comes very hard for many people. For those who have been "doers," it is a natural trap to continue "doing" after you become a manager. You use your people only as coolies to enable *you* to do more *doing*. Many men who build their own businesses from scratch often have a difficult time in learning to delegate. They are so accustomed to knowing every detail of what is going on, until they wake up one day and realize that the business has gotten too big for them to continue operating in that same manner. (Hopefully they discover it. And discover it in time.) Jeno

Paulucci in his book *How It Was To Make $100,000,000 In A Hurry* described this experience:

> For almost twenty years I was in complete control. I had built this thing from nothing and it was part of me, a one-man show. In the early days, before I began to delegate, I made all the decisions of any importance. . . . Then, almost before I knew it, we had a pretty big company on our hands—too big for me or anyone else to handle alone. So I . . . started to learn agonizingly, the technique of delegation.
>
> "Most business skills had come easy for me—but not this one. I wasn't good at delegation, but I made myself learn it. . . .

If you are working under someone who is telling you what to do—treating you like a coolie—"blow the whistle." Insist that you be told what you are responsible for, what your limits of authority are, what is expected of you and how you are to be measured.

> The successful people are the ones who can think up stuff for the rest of the world to keep busy at.
>
> —Don Marquis

■ You Can Be Given a Position—You Earn Status

Many young men are almost miraculously transformed overnight into different people when they are first promoted. One day a man is "Mr. Nice Guy." The next day he is acting more like management than management itself. He does not seem to realize that he was promoted because of the way he *was* yesterday, not the way he *is* today. Unfortunately, his business associates above, below and sideways are already focusing their attention on him to see if getting promoted "went to his head."

If there was ever a time for a man to be unassuming, perhaps a little more humble than usual, it is immediately following any kind of special recognition. It is at this point that your outward behavior can either "make you or break you" for a long time to come with the people on whom you must depend for your effectiveness.

Within any group there is interdependence. If you try to wear a position like a uniform, you invite long-lasting—if not permanent—resentment. There have been instances when an employee who is promoted or given new responsibilities is "killed" the first day from the standpoint of ever being effective. The deep wounds inflicted the first day might eventually heal, but the scar tissue remains, never to be forgotten.

A specific example: One of our employees was transferred from being the manager of one department, where he had been quite effective, to being manager of another department. The first day on the job, he took over the office which had been occupied by the man in the department who was to be his number two man, (the man who was the greatest potential key to his effectiveness). With great reluctance, the number two man moved out of the office which he had occupied for a long time and had liked very much.

You can guess the end of the story. The new manager was *never* effective from the first day. How could he expect to be able "to achieve results through other people" when he had thrown his number two man out of his old office on the first day? When he threw out the man, he threw out his own effectiveness. The number two man, consciously or unconsciously, destroyed the new manager's effectiveness with all of the people within the department. The new manager burned his bridge of effectiveness (in the form of his number two man) between himself and all of the rest of the people in the department.

What was my reaction to the new manager taking over the office of his number two man? Was I resentful? I was to the extent that I could mentally put myself "in the shoes of the number two man." *More importantly*, this incident told me a great deal about the new manager's ability to handle people. If this was the kind of judgment that I could expect, what was he likely to do in other situations requiring good judgment? I knew his future effectiveness would probably be destroyed and it was very unlikely that he could create a climate in the department in which his people would be motivated to do exceptional work. The man destroyed himself on the job and soon left the business of his own accord. He felt he was capable, but that he did not have any good people with whom to work.

A good test for the way you deal with the people who answer to you is to ask yourself: "Am I dealing with this person in such a manner that, if someday our positions were reversed, would I feel comfortable about how I had dealt with him when he answered to me?" If the answer is yes, you have passed the test. If the answer is no, you had better reassess your manner of dealing with people. This does not imply that you should not deal with your people firmly but rather that you should be fair.

Another important question is: If some day this employee becomes a customer or is otherwise in a position to have a major impact on our organization, can we look this person in the eye and know that we have dealt with him fairly in the past? This is a very practical question. I have been in this situation many times with ex-employees. I also have been in the position myself as a former employee of the IBM Corporation. I now am an IBM customer and have paid them over one million dollars over the last ten years. If I had not been dealt with fairly at IBM, I would not be one of their customers today. If you deal fairly with people, when they leave they are potentially some of your best salesmen without being on the payroll. An endorsement by an ex-employee is one of the best endorsements an organization can obtain.

We should not indulge in popularity contests in business. We should strive for respect. Managers who boast that they are "well-liked" by their people are indulging in a luxury that they cannot afford to concern themselves with until they have first gained the *respect* of their people.

At times when I have had the unpleasant duty of terminating a relationship with an employee, it has become obvious that there are some hard feelings on the part of the employee. I often will say, "You may not like me. I would like to have your friendship—but my real concern is to have your respect."

You can be given a position but you cannot be given "status" you have to earn it. And, particularly in a new situation, you need to proceed very cautiously in order that you do not star off "behind the eight ball." Test the water before you begin to assert yourself. Let people get used to you; do not overplay the management role. All of the people with whom you deal will respect you for it and you will have a good running start on your new responsibilities.

■ Completed Action—Personal and Staff

Never make a decision yourself, if you don't have to. When one of your men asks you a question, ask him what is the answer. There is only one answer to many questions, and, therefore, this method answers many questions before they are asked. It not only develops your men, but also enables you to measure their ability.

—Henry L. Doherty

When I was an inexperienced IBM salesman, I developed the very bad habit of constantly going to my manager with problems and asking, "What should I do?" One day my manager closed the door to his office and asked me to sit down. He handed me a one-and-a-half page write-up entitled "Completed Staff Action." He had gotten the write-up while he was in the army during the forties. The paper was written in military style and I will therefore paraphrase it as it would pertain to business or your personal dealings with others:

COMPLETED STAFF ACTION

1. "Completed Staff Action" is the study of a problem and presentation of a solution by a man to his manager, in such form that all remains to be done on the part of the manager is to indicate approval or disapproval of the completed action. The words "completed action" are emphasized because the more difficult the problem is, the greater the tendency to present the problem to your manager in a piecemeal fashion. It is your responsibility to work out the details. You should not involve your manager in the determination of those details. You may and should consult co-workers at your level and at lower levels in the organization. The recommendation, whether it involves the pronouncement of a new policy or affects an established one

should, when presented to the manager for approval or disapproval, be worked out in finished form.

2. The inexperienced man is often tempted to ask the manager what to do. This recurs more often as the problems become
more difficult. The impulse is accompanied by a feeling of
mental frustration on the part of the subordinate. It is so easy
to ask your manager what to do, and it appears so easy for him
to answer. Resist that impulse. You will succumb to it only if
you do not know your job. It is your job to advise your manager
what he ought to do, not to ask him what you ought to do. He
needs answers, not questions. Your job is to study, write, re-
study and rewrite until you have evolved a single proposed
action . . . the best one of all you have considered. Your manager
merely approves or disapproves.

3. Do not bother your manager with long explanations and
memoranda. Writing a memorandum to your manager does not
constitute completed staff action. However, writing a memorandum for your manager to send to someone else *does* constitute
such action. Your views should be placed before him in finished
form so that he can make them his views simply by his approval.
In most instances, completed staff action results in a single
document prepared for the approval of the manager without
accompanying comment. If the proper result is reached, the
manager will usually recognize it at once. If he wants comment
or explanation, he will ask for it.

4. The theory of completed staff action does not discourage
the writing of a "rough draft"; but the draft must not be a half-
baked idea. It must be complete in every respect except that it
need not be neat. However, a rough draft must not be used as
an excuse for shifting to the manager the burden of formulating
the action.

5. The "Completed Staff Action" theory may result in more
work for the man, but it results in more freedom for the manager
to do his own work. This is as it should be. Further, it accomplishes two things:

   a. The manager is protected from half-baked ideas, volu-
      minous memoranda, and immature oral presentations.

b. The subordinate who has a real idea to sell is able to inject his creativeness and ability into the responsibilities of the position that he holds.

6. When you have finished your completed staff action, the final test is this:

If you were the manager would you be willing to approve the suggested action that you have presented?

If the answer is no, take it back and work it over, because it is not yet completed staff action.

I was given the concept almost twenty years ago and since that time completed staff action has been a major fundamental in my business philosophy. I have a sign on my desk that reads, "What Do You Recommend?" At this point, I could remove the sign because the people who answer to me know that I expect completed staff action when they bring a problem to me. This is a very healthy discipline. When you adopt a policy of completed staff action, it will soon become obvious to your people. They will acquire the good habit of thinking through their own problems, and arrive at recommended solutions.

You can adopt this principle in meeting your own problems through "Completed Personal Action." Instead of acting impulsively, define the problem, preferably in writing. List the alternate solutions with the advantages and disadvantages of each. Then, recommend a solution to yourself on a logical basis.

Managers respond favorably when their subordinates follow this philosophy. In fact, I think completed staff action is perhaps THE most favorable indication that I receive from an employee.

Often what appears to be a problem disappears during the definition of the problem or in the listing of the possible alternate solutions. You will find that the answer becomes obvious before you complete the procedure. It is a case of approaching problems on a logical, unemotional basis.

Inherent in the theory of completed staff action is the fact that the recommended solutions to problems are determined at the lowest possible level at which they should properly be made. They are made where the action is, right on the firing line.

■ Getting to the Heart of the Matter

A man who is at the top is a man who has the habit of getting to the bottom.

—Joseph E. Rogers

The "two-dollar" word for getting to the heart of the matter is incisiveness. So for the sake of brevity in this chapter, let's call it that. The ability to get to the heart of the matter (incisiveness) is not necessarily something with which you are born. It is something that you can develop within yourself. It can be done largely on a mechanical basis.

The problem with being "incisive" is that the really significant or important factors are usually buried in a sea of irrelevant data. You must sift out that which is unimportant. The problem is compounded by the number of people involved in attempting to identify what it is that you are after and then arrive at the proper conclusions. You are also hampered by people who don't understand what it is that you are trying to accomplish and still will not understand after the matter is settled and the conclusions have been reached and explained to them. You will always find people who could be playing the piano downstairs in a house of ill repute and would not know what was going on upstairs. Unfortunately, there are far too many of them around.

You do not have to be the "expert" in the group to get to the heart of the matter. You can be the catalyst or the "coach." On many occasions I am in meetings where I know less about the subject matter or the situation than anyone else in the room. I will remain quiet until I get an indication that no one is going to assume the initiative and cut through all of the "crap" and get down to the bare bones. At this point, I will inject myself by first asking, "Gentlemen, will someone please define for me in about two short sentences what it is that we are attempting to accomplish?" I usually find that the conversation has gotten way off the main stream and that the thing we are trying to accomplish in no way resembles the current trend of the discussion taking place. My question usually brings the objective into focus. I will not give up until someone gives me a simple definition of what it is that we are after.

During this period, when the group is getting into agreement as to a concise definition of what it is that we are trying to accomplish, I often will remain quiet. This is particularly the case if I am less knowledgeable about the subject than are the others.

After having gotten a "fix" on our objective, I then ask the question: "What are our alternatives?"

Once the alternatives have been established, I take each one and ask: "What are the advantages and disadvantages of each alternative?"

Now that the advantages and disadvantages are determined, it is usually rather easy for the group to get into agreement as to the sequence of preference for the various alternatives. At this point, the answer is usually so obvious as to what should be done that no real decision has to be made. By following the above mechanical process, the answer is developed as the end result of a very logical process.

It is obviously more difficult for a group to get into agreement than it is for an individual to make a decision.

This same procedure for getting groups to be incisive also works effectively when you are thinking through a situation on your own.

Of the characteristics that a person MUST have to be successful, the ability to be incisive would have to rank near the "top." With many successes this has to be the real key.

Here are the steps in problem-solving that we have covered;
1. Define the problem very briefly.
2. List the alternatives.
3. List the advantages and disadvantages of each alternative.
4. Rank the alternatives as to preference.
5. Come to the most obvious conclusion.

■ Get It All Off the Bottom

When I was an IBM salesman we had a monthly report called "My Record." This report ranked all of the salesmen in the district based on their performance during the past month. My manager told me once that the goal was to get *everyone* off the bottom of the list, which of course was impossible. I have often thought about that "goal."

When I first went into business I was working alone and I was working long hours. After my time was completely filled, I would analyze my time to determine the least important thing I was doing which could be turned over to someone else. Then I hired my first employee, and gave him the least important work that could be delegated. After I filled my time again, I would ask myself the same question and would delegate a part of what I was doing to someone else. I would always be careful not to downgrade—but rather upgrade—what I was doing. In this way, almost as by geological pressure, I was pushed higher and higher, always upgrading. This was a wonderful experience for me and it is a habit that I continue to maintain. When I begin to get overloaded, I always ask myself "What am I doing that is least important that can be turned over to someone else?"

Often people become like a stagnant pond, with nothing coming in or going out. They fill their time and then say they cannot take on any more work because they have no more time. This results in a stand-off; a plateauing out in their growth.

The proper approach is to first delegate that part of your work which is least important. The business world does not like a vacuum and you will find that the time you freed by delegating part of your responsibility is quickly filled with more important work as you upgrade your standards of the type of work you do.

> I've never known of an instance in the history of our company where an executive unloaded responsibilities and duties on one lower in the ranks, that he did not find himself immediately loaded from above with greater responsibilities.
>
> —Arthur F. Hall

Not only can you use the principle of "getting it off the bottom" in regard to the work that you do, but you can also apply it to yourself, to other employees, and to analyzing situations. Let's take them one at a time.

Take a sheet of paper and draw a line down the middle. On the left side at the top of the page make a plus (+) sign. On the right hand side at the top of the page make a minus (—) sign. Then rank your strengths on the left side and rank your weaknesses on the right side. After you have done this, go to someone who knows you well and whose opinion you respect. Ask him to rank your strengths and weaknesses (without seeing your own analysis), and then compare his analysis with what you had listed. You may discover that others see things in you that you have not been able to see in yourself. After you are satisfied that you have a fairly accurate list, begin to work on those weaknesses that you can do something about. Start with what appears to be your greatest weakness. Perhaps it is a hot temper, using poor English, sloppy dress, undependable, always late, etc. Eliminating or neutralizing weaknesses can often be much more effective than trying to develop further a strength. It just depends on the individual.

The above procedure can obviously be used in analyzing other people and in counseling with them on where they need to improve. Ask them to list their strengths and weaknesses and then you compare them with your list, etc.

As to situations, list the good and bad points and then begin to hammer away at eliminating the bad points.—sales too low, costs too high, poor quality, slow schedules, etc.

When confronted with two courses of action I jot down on a piece of paper all the arguments in favor of each one—then on the opposite side I write the arguments against each one. Then by weighing the arguments pro and con and canceling them out, one against the other, I take the course indicated by what remains.

—Benjamin Franklin

■ Are You Getting the Message?

If there is any great secret of success in life, it lies in the ability to put yourself in the other person's place and to see things from his point of view—as well as your own.

—Henry Ford

Communication—or the lack thereof—is critical to success.

I talk and you listen (maybe) but are you hearing what I am trying to say? If I say to you that I like fish, and you say that you also like fish, are we communicating? Not necessarily. I might have in mind a big fish, filleted, on a plate with all of the trimmings; or perhaps I might be thinking about a large bass on the end of my fishing line. You may be thinking about something entirely different. You may have in mind an aquarium with a bunch of tropical fish swimming around. This is where the communication problem comes into play. Even if the conversation had been recorded and played back ten times to make sure that everything said was heard, we still would have had a communication problem.

One manager has a small sign on his desk which reads: "Every story has three sides, your side, my side, and the facts." Experience would indicate that this is a pretty accurate indication of the way that things usually are. Seldom is anything ever black or white. It usually ends up being a shade of gray. Whenever you are having a discussion with anyone about a subject and you are not in agreement, you can probably bet that you are not as right as you think you are, nor is the man with whom you are talking as right as he thinks he is. Somewhere in-between your two viewpoints is probably the way things really are. Herein lies one of the real keys to success. This is to make allowances for your own lack of objectivity . . . the other fellow's lack of objectivity . . . and sift out the facts.

When I'm getting ready to reason with a man, I spend one-third of my time thinking about myself and what I am going to say—and two-thirds thinking about him and what he is going to say.

—Abraham Lincoln

We seldom have perfect understanding—nor do we usually need it. But it is important that things from your side and things from my side look enough alike so that we can accomplish our objective.

As the size of the group of which you are a part increases, it becomes more of a challenge to maintain adequate communication. When an organization is small, communicating downward gets the emphasis. The manager or the owner tells the people under him what he wants done. Because of the small size of the organization it is relatively easy for him to make sure that it gets done. This is "one-way communication." As the size of the organization increases there is more of a need for "two-way communication" . . . first, communicating downward what is to be done, and then getting "feedback" as to how we are doing relative to our objectives.

Characteristically many small businesses are run by hard-nosed, autocratic type of managers. As the businesses grow, such managers often get into trouble, because their attitude discourages good two-way communication. Employees often feel inhibited in communicating upward. This is why it is always much easier to communicate downward than upward. For example, a manager will make damn sure that he understands a subordinate. He will ask questions, will tell the subordinate that he does not understand, etc. However, if the subordinate does not understand, he will think twice before saying so for fear that it will be interpreted as a sign of weakness or stupidity. This often results in an employee's "faking it."

Good communication is everybody's responsibility—manager and nonmanager alike. Sometimes a failure to communicate effectively can place you in jeopardy. True, good communication is your manager's responsibility—but you have the most to lose if your manager does not communicate to you effectively.

So consider the following: First, ask questions if there is any doubt in your mind as to the intent of the communication. Many people have the mistaken idea that the manager will think them stupid if they ask questions. I react in just the opposite manner. When people ask me questions, this says to me that they probably understand everything that I have told them except what they are questioning me about. Therefore, If I answer their questions and they indicate that they understand the answers I am fairly safe in assuming that they have gotten the message. However, sometimes I tell people to do something, then ask "Are there any questions?"—and they tell me no. I am not sure that they understand a damn thing I am talking about. In selling situations, particularly, I have often asked a question even when I knew the answer just to convey to the other party that I *did* understand everything but that one point. Instead of asking questions being a sign of weakness, I turn it into a strength.

> I attribute the little I know to my not having been ashamed to ask for information, and to my rule of conversing with all descriptions of men on those topics that form their own peculiar professions and pursuits.
> —Locke

The more successful a person becomes, the more he has the tendency to ask questions, some of which may sound elementary if not stupid. A successful man does not have to justify his ability. He is perfectly willing to stand on his past record, and has no concern for how stupid one of his questions may sound to someone else. Newer members of a group tend to be quiet rather than risk asking a stupid question. You can draw out people like this by asking some rather simple questions yourself in order to encourage them to speak out.

> No man really becomes a fool until he stops asking questions.
> —Charles P. Steinmetz

Memos have been grossly misused as an instrument of communication. A memo at best is one-way communication. A memo should be used not as a communicator but as a confirmation of communication, after an understanding has been reached. Some managers write memos to other managers whose offices are only a few feet away. It would be far better for the two managers to speak briefly, agree, and then confirm their understanding with a brief memo.

The tape recorder helps in establishing accurate communication. In our organization we tape most meetings, and I usually go back later and summarize the meeting from the tapes. It is interesting to note the different interpretation you may have of a meeting after you have had an opportunity to review a tape and go over some of the more complex points two or three times. The tape recorder can be an invaluable tool in meetings, calls on customers and prospects and even phone calls. A word of caution—as a courtesy and perhaps even from a legal standpoint—in taping calls, permission should be asked prior to the use of a recorder. Some people prefer not to have their comments recorded.

Another stumbling block to communication is vocabulary. If you use one word in a sentence that the receiver of the communication does not understand, he is very likely to miss the whole point. Extensive vocabularies can be the enemy of *good* communication. My personal interest in a good vocabulary has to do with understanding words when I see them in print, to use in crystallizing my thoughts, and to express myself to others in the clearest possible way. There is a vast difference between speaking properly and having a good vocabulary. You can speak properly without using words that most people would not understand. A person who uses words in communicating with the "average man" that the average man would not understand is only reflecting unfavorably on himself. When someone uses a word you are not familiar with, do not hesitate to ask him what the word means. You will both learn something. You will learn what the word means and he might learn not to use such difficult words without knowing the audience better.

There are also words that are peculiar to a particular profession but are foreign to most people. This is true in medicine, law, construction, data processing and in almost every other field to some degree. I have been rather effective as a salesman of computers and computer services for eighteen years. I attribute my effectiveness in a large measure to the fact that I do not have a strong technical aptitude. To understand the computer business, I have always had to reduce it to very simple terms and very simple language. In turn, I have sold other people by relating to them in the same simple language and they have been able to understand what I was saying. Whether you are actually "selling" or just trying to communicate your ideas to another person, you might try communicating as though you were talking with a ten- or twelve-year-old child. You may surprise yourself at your effectiveness. Not only will the person understand what you are saying, but he will also understand that you are not trying to give him a "snow job" as to how knowledgeable you are. This seems to be an occupational disease in the computer business to try to impress laymen with the industry. Perhaps it is true in your industry.

Two-way communication is not *always* best, it is just *usually* the best. To use a ridiculous example, if the building is on fire, one-way communication is the obvious answer . . . "Let's get the hell out of here!" Whenever speed is of great importance, one-way communication may be the answer. Most of the other reasons for using one-way communication are negative. For example, you may be wrong, but if so you do not want anyone to tell you that you are. You do not want to be confused with the facts. Use one-way communication if you want to look as efficient as an executive in a Hollywood movie or impress your girl friend. Also use one-way if you want to pass the buck. Then if things backfire you are not implicated. Like Pontius Pilate your hands are clean.

Use two-way communication whenever you want participation. You communicate out and then look for feedback to make sure that what you meant to say and what was heard are the same. For a person who understands how to really delegate two-way communication is vital. You are delegating authority and responsibility but not accountability. If you delegate and use one-way communication you are playing "Russian roulette" with the achievement of objectives.

Adolf Hitler was a good example of a type that often occurs in business on a much lesser scale (and hopefully with less severity). Hitler started off as a very effective communicator. He "read" the people in a marvelous way or he would never have been able to achieve the power that he ultimately did. He listened to the people in his party, built a powerful organization and was effective at waging war. As he became more successful he began to believe more strongly that he was incapable of error and he began to listen less. He got into trouble and crisis set in. The need for speed and fast action resulted in the continued use of one-way communication until he was ultimately destroyed.

Actually, toward the end Hitler did not communicate at all. The people had lost the faith. His military felt that he was insane, and when he talked, no one paid attention. This is not even one-way communication. All of us have been in a room with the radio on, and realized after a few minutes that we have not heard a word. This is true all too often in business. What we often refer to as communication is simply words in the air.

It's strange that, in business, one-way communication is used so often when two-way communication is so much easier. In one-way communication, you have to be precise and careful in order to attempt to get your message across. It has to be well-thought out and organized. All of this takes a great deal of time.

In two-way communication, you can keep it loose. You do not need to be as precise or do as much preparation or wait as long to begin to communicate. You get right at it. You explain it one way. If he is not getting the message, you try it another way. Then you ask the other fellow to summarize back to you what it is that you have told him. If he still does not have it, you explain it again, perhaps a different way. He asks questions which indicate the areas that are still not clear. You communicate back and forth until you know that you are on the same frequency. Once this is accomplished you can summarize your conclusions and then perhaps confirm them in writing with a memo (to confirm, not to communicate).

"Tracer" bullets show the gunner a lighted path so he can see if he is hitting the target. The difference between two-way and one-way communication is the difference between shooting tracer bullets—and knowing if you are hitting the target—or shooting regular bullets and not knowing what the hell you are hitting.

Organizing Your Time
and Yourself

IN THE SUMMER of 1947, when I was sixteen years old, I worked for a wholesale grocery company in Atlanta. It was shortly after World War II and chocolate bars and chewing gum were just beginning to be available again. Chewing gum was very hard to come by and we had to parcel it out, getting as much mileage as possible out of it by favoring our best customers.

To me, *time* is like the scarce chewing gum of those days. You cannot get all of it that you want, so you should expend it carefully where it means the most to you. Time is not a bottomless well. You have an inventory of time every day—twenty-four hours. We all do. There is nothing more democratic. You have just as much time as the president of the United States and the bum on the street—no more, no less. How well we succeed is largely a function of how well we use this inventory of time.

The first day on the job or in your new business you have plenty of time for everything. You have no customers; the phone is not ringing; you do not get any mail; no one is answering to you or asking you questions; there are no records to keep; your briefcase is empty. In short, you are Mr. Available. You do not have a time problem. Your problem is that as far as the business world is concerned, you don't exist. You start out on your first day with the feeling of being well-organized. There are no pressures on you.

In a short period of time you begin to realize that now your days are filled. Even worse, a lot is not getting done and you have customers to keep happy, prospects to call on, records to keep, mail coming in. Suddenly you realize that you are "snowed under." At this point many people begin to get in a rut, and if they progress at all it is very slowly. Inevitably they level off and eventually they begin to go downhill. If you put this on a chart it would look like a bell-curve;

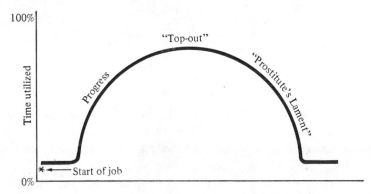

After the average person has "topped out" he begins to go down hill. He becomes the victim of the "Prostitute's Lament," which is that if you do the same thing for the same return long enough, you will ultimately do the same thing for less return.

You lose interest in the game. You begin to get swallowed up by the mountain of details that continue to make demands on your time. You never get around to doing the things that are really important to you.

But the Prostitute's Lament need not be your fate. There is a simple solution.—simple from the standpoint of defining the answer. The answer is to *give the gum to your best customers.*"

Sit down and begin to plan what you are going to do with your time inventory. Set objectives as to what you want to accomplish. Plan how you are going to accomplish these things with the resources that you have available through proper organization. Then establish control over your progress by setting up check points to determine if you are still on course and, if not, what it is that you can do to get back on course. This is an overview of what you should do.

> Most businessmen generally are so busy coping with immediate and piecemeal matters that there is a lamentable tendency to let the "long run" or future take care of itself. We often are so busy "putting out fires," so to speak, that we find it difficult to do the planning that would prevent those fires from occurring in the first place. As a prominent educator has expressed it, Americans generally "spend so much time on things that are *urgent* that we have none left to spend on those that are *important.*"
>
> —Gustav Metzman

■ Time Is a Full Bucket

Everyone keeps his "time bucket" full. There are no empty spaces in your time. Every day we fill up twenty-four hours doing something, whether it be working, playing, hobbying, watching T.V., staring into space or whatever.

Before committing your time to anything, ask yourself, "Am I willing to give up something that I am now doing in lieu of the commitment?" For example, if the Society For the Prevention of Cruelty to Whales calls you and asks if you will volunteer to work with them for one day six months henceforth, the natural tendency might be for you to say to yourself, "What the hell, I don't have anything planned for six months from today, so why not?" You have just fallen into the trap. Six months from today will come. It is ridiculous to assume that the day will be completely open. So it's a good idea to consider any time commitment—no matter how far off—as happening *tomorrow* . . . "If they wanted me to do this tomorrow or the next day, would I be willing to do this project in lieu of what I normally would be doing?" If the answer is no, turn them down. If the answer is maybe, then say to the Whale Society, "Check back with me two weeks before the day you need me and I will see how my schedule stacks up."

If a salesman calls me today and asks for an appointment next week, (assuming I am interested in talking to him) I will usually say, "How about this afternoon or first thing in the morning?" The reason is that by being careful with my time commitments, I find that there are several periods during the day when I am in the office working on a long-range project or perhaps doing paper work; and I could very easily squeeze in a discussion with a salesman or some other caller without disrupting my schedule. Also, when you see a person that day or the next it is much easier to gracefully bring the discussion to a close. It is easy to say "I am sure you can understand that I had not planned ahead on your coming out to see me today and I do have several other matters that I must take care of." If a salesman has had an appointment with you for two weeks, he may naturally expect that you are going to spend a great deal of time with him.

Let's assume that, when you suggest the salesman come in "today or tomorrow," he says he is booked up and can't get together until next week. Your reaction then is: "Fine. You call me next week at 9:15 AM on the day that you would like to see me or the day before you would like to see me and I feel quite sure I will be able to see you." You are telling the salesman the absolute truth. If you do not want to see him at all, tell him. Never succumb to making an appointment with someone whom you do not want to see—just because he asks weeks in advance.

This technique does more than enable you to use time effectively. It gives you greater flexibility in your schedule, because you have relatively few commitments ahead of you. Make a conscious attempt to commit yourself only during the current week. As of each Monday morning you will have very few time commitments for the week. (Carefully plan what you want to accomplish during the week—but don't make time commitments.)

When you are working under pressure, you can absorb the pressure more easily if you do not have an appointment calendar that looks like a time table for a milk-train. Too many people stay booked solid on their time with the result that some appointments have to be cut short before business is concluded because there is another appointment waiting. This means having to set up another appointment at a future date to conclude your business. It disturbs the continuity of the business to be transacted and calls for time-consuming review of what happened in the first meeting.

There are times when you schedule a thirty-minute appointment and get through in twenty minutes. What can you possibly get cranked up to do in ten minutes? This brings us to another device for using your time effectively: "batch processing your work."

"Batch processing" is a term used in data processing to describe the procedure whereby you process large amounts of data through perhaps ten different steps in an operation. Instead of taking each transaction or item through all ten steps to its completion and then going back and taking another through the same ten steps, you process all of the items through step one, then all of the items through step two, etc. The result is that you go through each step only one time and at that time you take all of the transactions you have through the step at the same time.

This process enables you to pick up a great deal of speed and efficiency in your everyday work. Instead of making phone calls off and on all through the day, you can sit down at one point and stay on the phone until you have completed the majority of phone calls that you have to make. Instead of calling your secretary into your office each time you run across something that she should handle, you batch process and wait until you have a stack of work to give to her all at the same time. This enables your secretary to use her time better. You will save your own time and that of subordinates—and establish better communication—if you can go to them with perhaps a list of ten things instead of running to them ten times. (Notice I said go *to* them. I rarely request that anyone who answers to me come to my office. They are closer to the firing line, so I go to them.)

It is equally as important that people batch process the matters they want to take up with the people to whom they report. It is very annoying for the same people to keep popping into the manager's office all day. Tell each co-worker that you would appreciate if if he would just jot down a list of the things he wants to discuss in order that you can cover as many different things as possible at one time. It usually doesn't take very long for them to get the message and once they get into the habit of batching what they want to talk about, they begin to use the same technique on others. This in turn improves their efficiency.

■ You've Got to Get Organized

Be methodical if you would succeed in business, or in anything. Have a work for every moment, and mind the moment's work. Whatever your calling, master all its bearings and details, its principles, instruments and applications. Method is essential if you would get through your work easily and with economy of time.

—W. Mathews

Staying well-organized is a real "sleeper" on the road to success. A man with average ability and drive who is well-organized often can run circles around those with more ability and a higher level of drive who are not well-organized. Being well-organized is not just desirable. It is *essential* to success. You can have everything going for you and fail because you are not well-organized.

The first step in being well-organized is to develop a "blue-print" or a "game-plan" of what it is that you want to accomplish.

The first fact that we must accept is that it takes time to stay organized. At this point, those who need most to be better organized roar in protest that they can not spare the time to *get* organized and *stay* organized. The paradox is that those who can spend the time to get organized probably do not have as great a need to do so. They probably have the time because of their good self-organization.

It is another case of cause and effect. Not having the time is the *effect* of the *cause* which is not being well-organized. Being *too* busy is not the problem, it is only a symptom of the problem.

No one is perfectly organized. It is a matter of degree. We can all improve to some extent. Good organization is a habit. Some people seem to be born with the knack, but those of us who had to learn it through practice can be equally as effective.

The three most powerful tools for being well-organized are: *common sense*, a *pencil* and a *tape recorder*.

If you are on the move and have a desire to succeed, it is a safe assumption that you are never at a loss as to how you can keep busy. You probably feel a sense of frustration at times by not being able to accomplish all that you would like to do.

If you follow the principles in the chapter on Management By Objectives, you will decide on your objectives and develop a plan for accomplishing them. This technique will automatically establish priorities for you.

Some people are born with better memories and more logical minds than others. However, by following mechanical procedures, you can keep up with the best minds available in staying well-organized. This is all that you have to do:

1. Purchase a loose-leaf notebook, plenty of paper, and some of those dividers with little tabs that enable you to label each section of the notebook between the divisions.

2. Take a sheet of paper and make a list of all the major types of activity in which you are regularly involved, both from a business and a personal standpoint. For example, some of the following are the activities that I use:

    a. Appointments

    b. Telephone calls to make

    c. Letters to write

    d. Prospect calls to make

    e. Each person (perhaps 5 or 6) with whom you have regular dealings on a variety of subjects—this could be your wife, children, boss, co-workers, subordinates, customers, etc.

    f. Things to follow up on

g. Things to think about or decide upon, including unsolved problems

h. Things to do "today"

i. Things to do whenever I get to them

j. Things to do as soon as possible

k. Miscellaneous notes on meetings, etc.

Customize your own list of major activities based on where you spend your time.

3. After making the list, alphabetize your various activities and label the tabs in your notebook accordingly.

4. Put several sheets of paper behind each type of activity and write down all of the things you can think of that you need to do under each activity.

5. As new things come up, *always* write them down. You will not always have the notebook handy, but be sure to jot it down on an envelope, candy wrapper, or whatever. Then, when you get back to your notebook, transcribe your notes into it. As you accomplish things that you have in your notebook, draw lines through them. Periodically, after most of the items on a page are scratched out, transcribe the remaining items on a clean sheet of paper. (Or, if you have a great deal of information to keep up with, instead of rewriting the items remaining to be done, cut them out with a pair of scissors, tape them on a clean sheet of paper and then xerox the paper. It saves a lot of rewriting and it comes out of the machine looking as good as the original with only those items yet to be done.)

6. In the front of the notebook, keep a single sheet of paper on which you list the specific things that you would like to accomplish during the current week, preferably ranked in priority sequence.

7. In the back of your notebook, insert a calendar with holes that fit the rings of the notebook. The calendar should have one page for each month, on which is a small block for each day of the month. On this calendar, record all of your specific appointments, deadlines, special events, meetings, out-of-town trips, etc., for as far into the future as it is practical.

If you have followed these seven steps, you should begin to

experience a great sense of relief, for you now have taken a giant step toward being well-organized. Within a week, staying organized with your notebook should be as much of a habit as brushing your teeth in the morning.

I was not well-organized until I developed this simple system. Here is what it has done for me:

1. I depend on my notebook like Linus in the "Peanuts" comic strip depends on his security blanket. Keeping my notebook handy is almost an obsession.

2. It has freed my mind from details and from trying to remember and categorize all of the things that I want to do.

3. I have time to think more creatively and to spend more time thinking about plans for the future rather than the details of today. It has therefore greatly improved my planning activity.

4. It has eliminated the frustration of feeling that I ought to be doing something that I am not doing and constantly going over and over in my mind those things to be done.

5. It enables me to "stay on the track" and to direct my efforts toward my highest priority objectives without being distracted by less important matters.

6. It has enabled me to use my time better with a greater return for the amount of effort required.

7. I can maintain an orderly work pace and enjoy my work because I am not constantly pressed for time.

8. I have been able to accomplish objectives more effectively through my subordinates. They know that when I ask them for something I make a note of it and will inevitably follow up if I do not receive a reply. It has become a very effective means of control. I know from observing other businessmen that once you slip up and do not follow through, people will henceforth try to "psych" you as to what you will remember and what you will forget. My subordinates know that, in essence, "I never forget."

9. I have gained a reputation for having an excellent memory, when actually my memory is only average. However, with my system, you can achieve the effect of an excellent memory even if you have a very poor memory. (Having a reputation for an

excellent memory and being well-organized is a significant factor at times with those who have an effect on your road to success.)

It would probably be safe to assume that many readers are saying to themselves that they are already well-organized and that they can not significantly improve their effectiveness by attempting to become better organized. Let me give you a little test. If you pass it I will agree that you probably do not need to be better organized than you already are .

The one day of the year that people are usually better organized than any other day is the day before they go on a two-week vacation. The day before vacation, most people get more done than they ever dreamed that they could do. They tie up all kind of loose ends, telephone calls, correspondence, etc. They are well-organized on this one day because of the constrictions of time. They have only so much time to accomplish a good many things before they leave town. Therefore, the first question on my two-question test is: Are you as well-organized all during the year as you are on the day before you would go on a two-week vacation? If the answer is no, brother, you just flunked the test. You *can be* more effective by being better organized, and until you come up with a better system, you might as well follow the one that I have outlined for you.

Next to the day before going on vacation, the next fourteen best-organized days of your year are probably the two weeks that you are on vacation. Many people can tell you almost to the minute what they will be doing during their entire vacation. The other fifty weeks of the year they rarely know from one day to the next what they will be doing. The second question, then, is: Are you as well-organized during the fifty weeks of the year that you are not on vacation as you are during the two weeks of the year that you are on vacation? If the answer is no, you need to get better organized.

When you are not well-organized, Parkinson's Law comes into effect and robs you of countless hours without your realizing it. Parkinson's Law is that "Work expands to fill the time available for its completion." This means that if you have one hour to pack a bag for a trip, it will take you one hour, if you have fifteen minutes, it will take you fifteen minutes to pack. If you have all day to pack, it will take you all day to pack. If you are not well-organized and have set forth a number of things that you want to accomplish each day, the few things that you think of to do during the day will expand to fill up much more time than would have been the case if you had allocated a reasonable amount of time for the completion of a task.

> A man would do well to carry a pencil in his pocket, and write down the thoughts of the moment. Those that come unsought for are commonly the most valuable, and should be secured, because they seldom return.
>
> —Bacon

■ Leave Yourself a Margin

Many people enjoy working under pressure. However, there is pressure and there is pressure. To set deadlines for yourself that require superhuman effort is suicidal. Some people will commit themselves to almost anything. They figure on everything going perfectly in order to meet a deadline, when in fact things almost never go as smoothly as anticipated. As a result, they stay up all night trying to meet a self-imposed deadline. Such a man will practically kill himself trying to accomplish a task—and still catch hell for being late. If he had given himself a margin, he would have been able to pace himself and accomplish the job with very little pressure and effort. He would have delivered when he said he would and been a hero.

Murphy's Law states that "If anything can go wrong, IT WILL." If you haven't learned this, you haven't been around very long. Things have a way of not going as planned. When you plan on optimum conditions with no allowance for something going wrong you are being unrealistic. Risk-assessment is not pessimism; it is realism. Pessimists are the most unrealistic people—but unrealistic projections are a major cause of failure

Often in the early days of our business, I would work all night, at least once and sometimes twice a week, out of the seven days that I was working. This problem that I created for myself was a result of several things, but a major contributing factor was that I had not learned to leave myself a margin.

The problem is compounded by the fact that the longer the hours you put in, the less effective you are per hour in what you are trying to accomplish. As the deadlines begin to close in, you begin to perspire regardless of the temperature of the room. Your thinking becomes muddled; you feel anxious. This isn't pressure, my friend, this is crisis.

I can not pinpoint the exact date that I got smart and started leaving myself a margin, but I think it was a result of a good "chewing out" I received from a good customer/friend of mine by the name of Marshall Mantler. He said to me, "Why commit yourself to deliver in two days and be a bum for delivering in three days, when you could commit to four days and then be a hero by delivering in three days?" This principle is so simple that in retrospect I am embarrassed to admit that I was ever so stupid. However, when I look around me and observe how other people operate, it is obvious that I had a lot of company.

You should plan to do more than you can actually get done in a day. If this sounds contradictory, let me draw a distinction. When I plan, I establish priorities, and there are some things that *must* be done today. There is a lot of difference between "Plan" and "Commitment." There are many instances in which I may *plan* to do something on a given day, but would not *commit* to it. I might commit to do something by Friday, but would plan to accomplish it by Wednesday. This leaves me a two-day margin in case of an unexpected turn of events. I often "overplan" what I think I can accomplish, but I very, very rarely "overcommit" to what I can accomplish.

It is human nature for people to negotiate the best deal they think they can get, not only in money, but in time. Often, when people are pushing you to meet a certain deadline, they are only trying to get the best deal that they can. They may not have any idea that you can really commit to what they are asking. You will also find that there are many people who leave themselves a margin. If I tell you that I want you to deliver to me by the fifteenth of the month, the chances are that I really need delivery three days later on the eighteenth. (Will my vendors please take note. I know what you are thinking. DON'T TRY IT!)

Here is the way that I would probably handle this type of situation today. If my customer said to me that he HAD to have delivery on the fifteenth and I knew that everything would have to go perfectly in order to deliver on the fifteenth, I would tell him exactly what the situation is. He is in business and he understands deadline problems and that things do not go as planned all of the time. I would say, "Look, you say that you have to have delivery on the fifteenth. I know that the only way I can deliver on the fifteenth is for everything to go perfectly and if fourteen years in this business has taught me anything, it is that things will probably not go perfectly. If, however, they do, I WILL deliver on the fifteenth. Assuming things do not go perfectly, what is the very latest that I can deliver to you and still give you a safe margin for the commitments that you have made?" I would also tell him that I want him to give me the most time that he can SAFELY give me in order that I can give him the best possible quality within the allotted time.

With this very honest approach, the customer will probably say, "My deadline is the nineteenth, and if your goods are not on my warehouse floor on the eighteenth, you can take your product and shove it." You have just bought yourself three days. Now comes the acid test.

Just because the customer has now given you until the eighteenth, this does not give you license to schedule completion on the eighteenth. You still have to make your plans based on finishing on the *fifteenth*. If you fall into the trap of eliminating your margin and schedule for completion on the deadline date of the eighteenth, sooner or later everybody loses. You get ulcers. You lose a customer or at least perhaps create a "credibility gap." Once you create the credibility gap it takes a lot of good work to build yourself back up to where you were.

This is equally applicable—and perhaps more significant—in the case of a man dealing with his manager. Chances are his manager will have a greater impact on his future than will a customer. If you create an environment in which your manager cannot depend on you to do what you are supposed to do when you are supposed to, your days are probably numbered. Not being dependable is a cardinal sin in business. Being dependable is like being pregnant—either you are or you aren't. There is no such thing as being a "little dependable."

■ It's Not the Hours that Count

Why is it that so many people try to equate hours expended on a project with results? Many people feel self-righteous about working long, hard hours. They delight in telling their friends about the time they are putting in. Overtime gives them a real sense of accomplishment. Then they find that the boss has little interest in long hours. He wants results. I have no idea of how many hours the key people in our company are putting in. I concern myself with their hours only if I feel that they are putting in too many, and affecting their health and efficiency on the job. I have often told people that I do not care if they work only half a day. What I am interested in is results. That is how I measure people, not by the number of hours they put in.

If you do not agree with this position, try this test. When you buy a product or service, (like a cleaning establishment to clean your suit) do you concern yourself with how much labor or effort goes into providing you with that product or service? If you do, you are a rare bird. Most of us concern ourselves with what it is going to cost us. We are willing to pay consistent with the value received, not on how long it took to provide the value. For some reason, many people who concern themselves with value received when *paying for it*, do not seem to be able to use the same yardstick when they are *being paid* for value received.

You have reached another plateau in your maturity the day you can quit relating to the number of hours that you put in and instead concentrate on the results that you can provide. When you are doing this you have made a giant step toward making *your* objectives compatible with those of the organization.

If you deal with customers in the outside world, you know

that this is where your results are really measured. The first time you tell a customer "I'm sorry that we don't have your work ready, but I have been putting in a lot of hours on it," your customer will teach you a lesson with a lot more force than I am able to do on the printed page. Your customer will tell you that he really does not give a damn how long you have been working, he wants to know when he is going to get delivery.

Well done is better than well said.

—Benjamin Franklin

■ Stay Loose

Be sincere. Be simple in words, manners, and gestures. Amuse as well as instruct. If you can make a man laugh, you can make him think and make him like and believe you.

—Alfred E. Smith

We all know people who have been very successful who are referred to as being "strictly business." It's hard to knock it if it works, but I do wonder if people who are strictly business have really learned to enjoy the game. Not only do I feel that if you are going to play the game you might as well enjoy it, but I think that there are some practical reasons for keeping it loose in business.

Part of the myth surrounding business is that it is a cold, calculating "dog-eat-dog" environment. It is not that way at all. People who view business this way are seeing only a reflection of their own attitude. I am reminded of the story about the traveler who inquired of the beggar on the outskirts of the strange town as to the type of people he could expect to find in the town. The beggar asked the traveler what kind of people there were in the town from which he came and the traveler replied that they were bad people. The beggar told the traveler that he could expect to find bad people when he entered the strange town. Another traveler came along and asked the beggar the same question. Once again the beggar asked the traveler about the type of people who were in the town from which he came. The traveler replied that they were all good people. The beggar then told the traveler that he could expect to find the same kind of people in this town. (It does make you wonder why the beggar had to beg for a living if he was so damn smart.) So it is with business or anything else. What we often see is just a reflection of our own distorted attitudes.

Business is made up of people . . . the same people you go to church with, meet on vacations, have over to your house, play golf with, etc. They do not turn into robots the minute they enter the world of business.

Recently I talked with a man who had been a purchasing agent. He took the position that when he was a purchasing agent, his buying policy was strictly P.D.Q., meaning price, dependability, and quality. He said that any salesman who had tried to motivate him into buying was wasting his time, inasmuch as his buying procedure was strictly mechanical. I disagreed with the gentleman. I said that the only mechanical part of his buying procedure was *price*; and that the other two considerations, *dependability* and *quality*, were very subjective in nature. He probably saw the amount of dependability and quality that he wanted to see based on the impact that the salesman had on him.

Professional athletes will tell you that they play better when they are loose. When they get "tensed up" they do not play as well. This is why they make a conscious attempt to stay relaxed while playing. So it is in business. When a salesman is tense and nervous he makes the buyer uncomfortable. The prospect becomes so absorbed in the salesman's nervousness that he pays little attention to the sales story.

In dealing with people, whether you are selling or not, always search for some common ground. This is the warm up period. In any type of sport, the players always warm up before they get down to the game itself. A warm up period is useful almost any time that you are going to engage in a conversation with anyone with whom you have not previously established a relationship. Very often a warm up is also desirable with people you already know.

It is easy to establish a relationship on common ground because there are hints all around you. When I call on someone whom I have not met, the first thing I usually do is to ask the man where he is from. (In Atlanta, most adults are usually from someplace other than Atlanta.) This has been effective for me because I have been around most of the United States and usually know something about the area from which the man came. The easiest way to find common ground is to look around as you enter his office. He will usually have all kinds of things that represent his interests. For example: If he has books, notice the subjects. Pictures on the wall tell a lot, as do mounted fish and game, mementos from his school, civic clubs, the early days of his business, his children, sports of different kinds. You may think that this is establishing a relationship on a superficial basis, but I would disagree. All of us seek out others with whom we have common ground and can communicate. I do not look for common ground in an attempt to "butter up anybody." I do it with whomever I meet, including salesmen who call on me. It is worth the investment in time because it helps to establish a good relationship. It tells the man that you are interested in him as a person.

Let me give you a concrete example. I was the guest speaker at an IBM seminar in Endicott, New York. While in Endicott, I stayed at the Homestead, an establishment owned by the IBM Corporation. In the dining room there are several round tables which seat eight people each, and you usually dine with seven people whom you have never seen before. At dinner one night there was a gentleman at the table who had said very little during the meal. About the time dessert was being served, I noticed from this gentleman's name tag that he was from New York, and I asked him if he was a fan of the New York Knickerbockers basketball team. I hit the "jack-pot." He lit up like a Christmas tree. As it turned out he had spent a great deal of time as a basketball referee and was currently coaching a basketball team of young boys who had won several championships. Soon, others who were also interested in working with young boys in sports joined the conversation. The gentleman who previously had said nothing was now the center of attraction in telling about his basketball activities. He was having a wonderful time. I honestly believe that after I had established this common ground I could have sold him a box of broken beer bottles. I won him over by asking one question. Then I just sat back and listened.

Another very important tool for keeping people relaxed and enjoying the game is *humor*. By humor, I do not mean joke telling. I resent it when someone whom I do not know calls on me and starts telling jokes. This serves no worthwhile purpose. He is not establishing common ground. He is only trying to soften me up, but it works in reverse. The kind of humor I am talking about has to do with seeing the light side of things, talking to a man as freely and with as much humor as you would if you had known him for a long time. Some people have a knack for using humor very effectively, others do not. If you obviously do not have the knack, don't press it, but you can still keep the conversation in a light vein by talking to him as though he were a long time friend.

When I was a young IBM salesman, I would play a mental game when I called on anyone who was very imposing or who, for some reason, caused me to feel uneasy. I used to develop a mental picture of the man sitting there in his underwear, or picture him in dirty clothes sitting in a fishing boat with me on a lazy summer afternoon. The picture helped me to mentally pull him off his pedestal so that I could feel comfortable in talking with him.

There is another important reason that you should develop a knack for seeing the light side of things. As you progress up the ladder there will be times when things pile up on you; when you are spending your hours in Gethsemane. It is in times like these that you almost have to learn to laugh to keep from crying. I have developed a knack for a kind of self-hypnosis. When things really start piling up and I cannot see daylight, I simply dismiss the problem from my mind until the appointed time comes for me to address myself to it. A simple example: if I know that two weeks from today I am scheduled to go through an unpleasant hour in the dentist's chair, I dismiss it from my mind until the time arrives for me to keep the appointment. Otherwise, the anticipation becomes much worse than the act itself. The day that I learned to do this was the day that I became much more effective as a public speaker. I no longer became nervous over having to make a speech sometime in the future. I prepared my subject matter but would not allow myself to even think about being nervous over the speaking engagement. People can be very well-prepared for a talk, but become so tense in anticipation of getting up before an audience that when the time for the talk arrives, they freeze up and "flop." A mental game you can use here to overcome "stage fright" is to pretend that all of the people in the audience owe you money, or that they are all your employees, relatives or any other group before which you would not be nervous.

Dismissing things from your mind is what psychologists call "repression." It is the act of eliminating from your mind that which your mind disapproves. Although repression is a form of defense mechanism, you can use it in a positive way to dismiss that which gives you no benefit to think about and that which your mind disapproves of. (Try it! You'll like it!)

When I was an IBM salesman, we were encouraged by the company to always call on the top man wherever possible. I became impressed by the fact that the higher in the organization the men were, the more they seemed to be relaxed, friendly, and able to see the humorous side of things. I first deduced that they were "loose" because they were at the top. After several years in business, I discovered that I had been 180 degrees wrong. They were not loose because they were "at the top." They were at the top because they were loose.

> The sense of humor is the oil of life's engine. Without it, the machinery creaks and groans. No lot is so hard, no aspect of things is so grim, but it relaxes before a hearty laugh.
>
> —G. S. Merriam

■ The Sharks and the Porpoises

Two or three years ago in our company, a man who had been doing a fairly effective job was moved to another department to work with a man who had been doing an effective job. It was like trying to mix oil and water. They were at each other's throats all of the time, and finally it was necessary for us to put them in different departments.

A few months later I was reminded of this situation when I was at Marineland Studios, north of Daytona Beach, Florida. At Marineland, the sharks are kept in one tank and the porpoises are kept in another. Any time that they are put together in the same tank, they fight to the death. The porpoise will usually kill the shark. The guide explained that porpoises are usually easy going and love to be around people. Sharks are just the opposite; among their other characteristics they have very little use for people. As I listened to him it occurred to me that we had tried to put a porpoise in the same tank with a shark with the inevitable result that they battled until there was only one left.

I have thought of the sharks and the porpoises many times since then whenever we started shifting people around and I have been conscious of trying not to put the sharks in the same tank with the porpoises.

There is a technique, widely used in management development, called the Managerial Grid. It was developed by Robert Blake and Jane Mouton. The purpose of the grid is to measure on one hand a person's concern for people (the degree of empathy that he has) as opposed to his concern for production. Either extreme is undesirable. A person who has too high a regard for people will give away the store if you have him in the sales department. If he is a manager, all of his people will love him but it is questionable that he will ever get any work turned out in his department. On the other hand, if he is at the other extreme and all he cares about is production with very little regard for people, you will have just as much of a problem. He will probably have constant turnover in personnel, a very low level of motivation in his people and his chances of remaining a manager will be slight.

Whenever you are considering working with someone, remember the sharks and the porpoises. Make sure that your relative regards for people and production are not so diverse that you will not be able to work effectively together.

Education—
Formal and Otherwise

The young man who has the combination of the learning of books with the learning which comes of doing things with the hands need not worry about getting along in the world of today, or at any time.

—William S. Knudsen

THE EDUCATIONAL level of people in this country continues to rise. It is assumed more and more that a young man starting out in his career will have a college education. Whether this much college education is really needed is a controversial subject. Many people have very strong feelings about it.

I feel that anyone who can possibly obtain a college education should do so; but I do *not* feel that it is *essential*. A college education is *desirable*. There are many instances where people continue to become highly successful without a college degree. In fact, *not* having a college education *has* some advantages which are worth considering. Some of these advantages are as follows:

144

1. Many people, when they graduate from college, feel that they are educated and that their learning process is largely over. They have a false sense of complacency about how much they know. They do not realize that all they have obtained thus far is the foundation for becoming educated in the real world.

2. A great deal of what you learn in school is theory. However, theory is of no particular value in becoming successful if not put to use. Unapplied knowledge is only information. Some college graduates view theory as an end in itself, rather than a means to an end.

3. Schooling takes time. A college education can cost you at least four years during which you could have started your business career.

4. A college education makes some people feel that it is a little above them to indulge in just plain "hard work," and that it would be degrading for them to "get their hands dirty." In the early days of my business, I spent time, among other things, driving the truck. Some college graduates might not want their old fraternity brothers to see them driving a truck.

5. A college education can create psychological barriers between people who have been to college and those who have not. Some people have inferiority complexes—either consciously or unconsciously—about not having a college education. This becomes an inhibiting factor in establishing good communications between college and noncollege men.

6. Some people "burn themselves out" in college. They seem to have given of themselves in college to the extent that by the time they start on their careers they are not very effective. It is a lot like runners in a long-distance race. They do not start off at full speed. They start off at a comfortable speed and pace themselves carefully. Then when they get to the "home stretch," they turn on the steam.

7. At times college graduates feel that they have a slight edge over their noncollege co-workers. This complacency, cou-

pled with the feeling of the noncollege man that he has to drive all the harder to compete with his college-educated counterpart, can spell real trouble for the college man in a competitive situation. Graduates of "the school of hard knocks" are not to be taken lightly.

8. Noncollege men may openly resent college graduates. Many college men served in the armed forces and trained under noncoms who had it in for the "college boys." There were plenty of moments when they had their doubts about the advantages of a college degree. The same thing can hold true with your superiors, subordinates, co-workers, people you are trying to sell, etc. Unfortunately, this resentment is often a closely-kept secret. You may think that you have their support; but consciously or unconsciously they are very much against you.

9. Some college graduates who have been "big men on the campus" suffer a letdown afterwards. They were active in student affairs. They held positions of leadership. All of this, plus a good scholastic record, makes them think that when they go into a business they will practically be running the place. The rude awakening and the letdown occur when they realize that their "sheepskin" is only their ticket into the ballpark; and that management is not too impressed with their ideas of revolutionizing the business. They find themselves relegated to a rather lengthy management training program without any authority to implement their brilliant ideas. Referring to a graduate who had just joined his organization, a friend of mine told me that he thought the young man would be all right as soon as he "unlearned" some of the things that he had picked up in college.

At this point you may be asking yourself, "Why go into all the disadvantages of a college education?", particularly for readers who have already graduated and are in business. I point out these disadvantages for the reason that I feel that you must be aware of these pitfalls and make allowances for them accordingly. I hope to be able to point out how the disadvantages can be turned into advantages, or at least be neutralized.

I feel that I am qualified to talk from both sides of the street. I am a college graduate; but I did not graduate from college until 1959, eleven years after I started. This was five years after I left IBM and two years after I started my own business. I believe that I have experienced the best of both worlds and feel quite fortunate to have been able to obtain a college degree long after I had embarked on a business career.

Here are some of the advantages of a college education—with comments on how some of the disadvantages can be turned into advantages:

1. Your college degree is one of the first ways that people have of judging you when you embark on a new career. It tells the company that you do have an education, that you stuck in there and didn't quit. The way that you handle the fact that you do have a college education also tells people something. If, for example, you act as if you think the world owes you a living, this will be taken into consideration. In some ways a college education is a cross that you must bear.

2. College creates a disciplined environment for learning. This is true of any type of school. I have heard people say that they do not have to go to church to worship God. This is certainly true, but church creates an environment which is conducive to worship. Likewise, a college or any type of school creates a disciplined environment that is conducive to learning. Many people do not exercise the self-discipline to learn on their own. They need the atmosphere of a classroom environment. Although I feel that most of what I have learned has been on my own and not in a school, I find that occasionally attending a school of some type is a good change of pace. I always derive a great deal of benefit from it.

3. College gives you perspective. It enables you to see the "big picture." You get exposure to many facets of business you would not get in many business situations. It enables you to see the role of accounting, law, finance, cost, marketing, management, etc. You are exposed to the theory, which usually precedes practice.

4. You learn to study and to read books. You discover the mechanics of the learning process. You begin to approach learning on a logical basis. You develop good learning habits, including the taking of notes and the marking of passages in books that are of special significance to you. Learning is largely practice. College gives you a tremendous amount of practice and keeps you under enough pressure to move along at a rapid pace.

5. College has a tendency to make you raise your sights, to realize that you can be much better than you are. It creates the motivation of self-fulfillment, the highest goal of man. It is an enriching experience that creates a growing awareness of many new things, and it helps a person to establish true values in life.

6. It provides you with greater momentum once you get out and embark on a career. Often the head start that non-college men have on their careers is soon overcome by college men by virtue of their college training.

7. Writing reports and speaking on your feet in front of groups helps you to become more articulate and aids in communicating with others.

8. It is a vehicle for a person to become "well-rounded" through being exposed to a variety of subjects other than those having to do with his career interests. For example, you will learn about history, English, language, chemistry, geology, physics, etc.—subjects that a person would not be exposed to in the pursuit of a career.

9. College helps a person to find the "thing" he wants to do. It provides the opportunity for a person to enter many fields that would not be available to him without a college education such as medicine, law, engineering, dentistry, physics, etc.

We have looked at some of the advantages and disadvantages of formal education. College is highly desirable, particularly when a person can take a college education in his stride and learn to neutralize some of the disadvantages. People who "wave the flag" of having been to college are just asking for trouble. I never have believed in wearing a college ring. They are often taken the wrong way by noncollege men. I always cringe when I hear a businessman start talking about his college fraternity, I wonder how many noncollege men are sitting there thinking, "Yeah, you jerk, while you were cavorting around in the fraternity, I was working my can off."

Don't get me wrong. You should not be ashamed of the fact that you *went* to college, but *went* is the past tense and that is where it belongs—in the past. Quit trying to relive your college days. People with whom you work will get the message, and they will respect you for the fact that you do not make a big deal over it and are able to communicate with men at all levels.

Formal education can be valuable—but by far the most important element of your education is the continuing part that is informal in nature. A formal education is like the foundation of a building. The biggest part of the whole structure is the building itself. Informal education is like the building. It is where all of the action really takes place. It is what you can see. It takes much longer to build. It is the part that has the big "pay off." They never rent out the foundation of a building.

It is very difficult to tell anyone how to get an informal education. However, there is an excellent summary chiseled on the five steps leading up to the IBM training center in Endicott, New York. The words are "Read, Listen, Discuss, Observe, Think." This is what education is all about.

What makes your informal education such a meaningful, valuable, continuing experience is that everyday you are working in the laboratory of your career, where you learn by trial and error—often for high stakes—and for keeps.

Fortunately, in many job environments people are forced to practice four of the five basic avenues of informal education: listen; discuss; observe; think. But the one left out is possibly the most important—*reading*.

Someone once said that a man who *does not* read is no better off than a man who *cannot* read. Reading in essence enables you to listen to the greats of all ages on any subject of your choosing. The more you read, the easier it becomes, the more you absorb, and the more you want to read other material. Buy books when you can afford it, rather than checking them out of the library. Mark them up. Underline passages that impress you. Make notations all through your books of things that the various passages bring to your mind. Some books you will read one time; others you will review until they are "dog-eared." Repetition is truly a key to learning and remembering. By reviewing a book after you have read it, you will absorb a great deal more than you did the first time through. By only reading the underlined passages and your notes you can review a book quickly.

Reading gives you an edge by helping you develop a philosophy toward your life or career that is a composite of *your* thinking and the thinking of the best minds in your field of endeavor. For example, I am a great disciple of Peter Drucker. Drucker is a famous business philosopher and although I have never met him, he has had a profound effect on my business life. If I find myself confronted with a dilemma, I tap on the philosophy of Drucker or the experiences of other men of business whom I have confidence. This does not mean that you should copy the thinking of authors of the books you read. I have developed a philosophy that is really not identifiable with any specific person but with which I feel comfortable. On some things, perhaps, I am right; on others, perhaps, I am wrong. Some of the things I write about you may embrace as part of your philosophy. I may have gotten them from someone else. I think it is to the reader's advantage that most authors are like "Robin Hood" in a way. They "rob" good ideas from those who are rich in thought and give them to those who are more poor in thought. Of course, you do not really rob ideas. You can not take them away from someone. The great thing about ideas is that if I have an idea and you have an idea and we swap ideas, we each end up with two ideas. A large part of the motivation for my writing this book is the sense of self-fulfillment that I get from being able to pass on to you what I have absorbed from others.

Some people say they can't improve their chances by reading because they have not done much reading since they left school. They feel that it is not possible for them to read many books.

They are wrong. No matter how much a person might have read, or will read in the future, he reads it all "one page at a time." Think about it. Confucius said that "a journey of a thousand miles starts with but a single step." A single page is like a single step, and each step takes you a little farther. The farther you go the more you get interested in the journey. The journey gets easier and you begin to quicken your pace. As you continue your journey, you crystallize in your own mind the paths that you can take to be successful; the areas of your greatest interests become clear.

You may find that what you read goes through a cycle. When I was in my early twenties I read books on the lives of successful businessmen and successful businesses. As I developed more of an interest in the sales field, I began to concentrate on books having to do with salesmanship. When I began to think about starting a business, I started reading books on operating small businesses and on business management. I find that most of my business reading now has to do with motivation, professional management of larger organizations, and business philosophy.

When we consider reading and business success, it is hard to determine which is cause and which is effect. As you become more successful, you read more, which in turn spurs you on to more success which in turn inspires you to want to improve yourself by reading more, and so on, and so on.

He that loveth a book will never want a faithful friend, a wholesome counselor, a cheerful companion, an effectual comforter. By study, by reading, by thinking, one may innocently divert and pleasantly entertain himself, as in all weathers, as in all fortunes.

—Barrow

■ When You Lock Your Desk—Don't Lock Your Mind

It would do the world good if every man in it would compel himself occasionally to be absolutely alone. Most of the world's progress has come out of such loneliness.

—Bruce Barton

Watch people as they leave work for the day. It is easy to spot the people who have locked up their minds at the same time they locked their desks. The people who are moving ahead and love what they are doing almost invariably leave their offices with briefcases, envelopes, papers, etc. It would be as unnatural for them to leave the office without a briefcase as it would to leave without their shoes.

Most people who take work home with them do not do so because they have to, or because they are in a crisis situation. *They like to work.* Unfortunately, the ever-present briefcase adds fuel to the fire in the myth of the "overworked executive."

Many people lock their minds when they lock their desks. They make sure there is no danger that a creative thought might creep into their minds on the way to work and back. They are very careful to turn on their car radios immediately after they have turned on the ignition. (If you do this try *not* turning on the car radio particularly on the way *to* work—or at least turn the volume down so that the radio is only a background to your thinking process.)

The time it takes you to go to work in the morning may be the most valuable time that you spend during the day. You are fresh, in privacy, and have no interruptions. You can think about your work day and any decisions that you plan to make. Often you will find that you decide on a different alternative than one chosen the previous day during the heat of battle at the office.

When I hike in the Great Smoky Mountains of North Carolina and Tennessee, I always enjoy the spectacular views. From the tops of mountains you get beautiful views of the valleys. From the valleys you get beautiful views of the mountains. This is the way it is with our careers. In order to get perspective, we need to get away from the job environment where we can see it with more objectivity. It is during these periods of objectivity when you are out of the job environment that you will probably make the real big decisions and do your most creative work. Then you move back into the main stream of the job environment to implement these decisions. Here are a few examples.

President Nixon has earned the reputation of being one of the hardest working presidents that we have had in modern times, and yet he spends a great deal of time at his homes in Florida and in California. He will also frequently go to Camp David outside of Washington to work on State of the Union messages, make decisions, etc.

William Zeckendorf, who built a tremendous real estate empire, got one of his best ideas while standing on a beach in Hawaii fishing. In his autobiography, *Zeckendorf*, he relates the incident:

> As the pieces and the arithmetic began to dovetail, I forgot my fishing or even where I was until I suddenly realized I was standing on a Hawaiian Beach, in water up to my ankles, with a useless rod and reel in my hands. I went into the house, and in the course of two hours on the telephone I began to make the first application of what was to become known in the trade as the Hawaiian Technique.

Conrad Hilton, in his book *Be My Guest* tells how he conceived the idea of buying the largest hotel in the world while riding on a train from Albuquerque:

> I remember distinctly it was on the train from Albuquerque where building had just begun that a daring new idea popped into my head.
> In my wallet still was the clipping of the "greatest of them all," New York's Waldorf Astoria. I knew she was way beyond me then. But there was another one, the largest hotel in the world, the Stevens in Chicago.

Don Mitchell, an outstanding businessman, who has been president of General Telephone and Electronics Corporation and board chairman of General Time Corporation, Sylvania Electric Products, Inc., and the American Management Association, had the following to say on this subject in his book *Top Man*:

> I have found it a very desirable technique to get away from it all and go to the mountains (often with my team) or anywhere far removed from the office. It is in this sort of environment that one can think and dream. A number of progressive companies also employ this

process. . . . Management critics have often dismissed such retreats as a form of boondoggling—the expense paid vacation. I believe that they miss the point completely, for a manager with many daily problems and "fire drills" simply cannot spend the time he needs to think intelligently about the future unless he can isolate himself for awhile.

In his book *How It Was To Make $100,000,000 In A Hurry*, Jeno F. Paulucci of the Chun King Corporation fame, made the comment:

"The thought came to me in an airplane, which is where I get most of my ideas."

In the last five years I have traveled extensively over the United States on business and pleasure, have attended many trade association meetings, fulfilled speaking engagements, etc. I have done more creative thinking about my business affairs during these trips than I ever would have in my office. I invariably come back anxious to try out some new ideas or new approaches to situations that have occurred to me while my desk was locked, but my mind was not.

It is not always easy to detach yourself from the day to day "doing" at the office and get to a vantage point from which you can view things more objectively. In January 1971, my good friend Robert Olsen of Detroit and I went snowmobiling in the upper peninsula of Michigan for about four days over a long weekend. We took with us bulging briefcases and at night we would sit around and have long discussions about business. One night Bob made a comment that has stuck in my mind. He said that he had "a guilty feeling of NOT DOING." He said that at times when he was away on a trip such as the one we were on, he felt somewhat guilty because he had the feeling that he should be back at the office "doing something."

Many people do not have much chance to get away from the office. However, most people take vacations. They go away on weekends and holidays. These times give you a chance to lock your desk and open your mind. Some of my friends find it hard to understand why I enjoy fishing—they feel that because I am extremely active, fishing would bore me. On the contrary, I love it. I usually go on a day during the weekend, and although the body has gone fishing, the mind has not. I have thought through some of my better creative efforts while sitting in a fishing boat with my father-in-law, Julian Still.

> Spend some time alone and learn to develop your personal resources.
> —Alexander Reid Martin

■ Let 'Em Depend on You

> There are admirable potentialities in every human being. Believe in your strength and your youth. Learn to repeat endlessly to yourself: "It all depends on me."
>
> —André Gide

Dependability is not a desirable trait in becoming successful. It is an *indispensable* trait. If you can not be depended upon, your chances of success are very remote.

Fortunately, you can develop this characteristic even if you are not now very dependable. Also, as is the case with many characteristics, when you start being dependable people will begin to forget the days when you were not. The action is now and tomorrow, not yesterday. In the past you may have been unpunctual; you may have procrastinated; you may have been indecisive. These are enemies of dependability—but you can defeat them.

Let's break dependability down into three parts: *Being punctual* means doing things when you said that you would do them, being places when you said that you would be there, etc. *Being decisive* means that you do not procrastinate, that you make decisions *when* you are supposed to make them and that you do not put off doing those things that you are supposed to do. The third element and most important element is the attitude of others toward you—that you *will do what you are supposed to do*, or that which you are capable of doing.

Punctuality is basically just a habit. Being punctual, though it is important, is of less importance than the other two elements of dependability. The importance of being punctual is not in the positive sense, but in the negative sense. You will not get a lot of mileage out of always being on time or doing things when you said that you would do them. People expect this. If, however, you are never on time and always late in delivering that which you had agreed on, people will sure as hell begin to wonder about your dependability.

> Nothing inspires confidence in a business man sooner than punctuality, nor is there any habit which sooner saps his reputation than that of being always behind time.
>
> —W. Mathews

Cocktail lounges in airports have tried to devise a mechanical method of making sure that people are punctual in leaving the bar to catch their flights. They usually move the clock ahead by fifteen minutes. However, the people who are habitually late, not to be outdone by this deception, make allowances for the fact that the clock over the bar is fifteen minutes fast. If the plane leaves at 8:00 P.M., they will not leave until the clock reads 8:10 P.M. They therefore still manage to miss their flights. There is no mechanical way to become punctual. You simply must decide that you are going to quit being late and to quit *not* doing things on time. You have to become realistic about how long it will take to get places and do things; and allow for a margin of error.

Being punctual is of the lowest priority in dependability because it is better to accomplish what you are supposed to do, even if late, than it is to always be on time, but never prepared once you get there. Howard W. Newton said that "People forget how fast you did a job—but they remember how well you did it."

Trying to get credit for being on time is like trying to get recognition for having remembered to tie your shoes this morning. Now that you have decided to start being punctual (that's all it takes), let's talk about procrastination, or rather *not procrastinating*.

For openers, procrastination is often the reason that we are not punctual. We put off doing what we are supposed to do until we get into a crunch and are not able to complete our objective in the allotted time.

Why do we procrastinate? Primarily because of uncertainty, the lack of information or something else that keeps us from making a decision to act. It may be a lack of knowledge, confidence, initiative, goal direction, concentration, creativity or imagination. If you find yourself in a position where you are obviously procrastinating or being indecisive, you should first "pinpoint" that which is preventing you from taking action. Once you have taken this step, you are now in a position to attack the cause for procrastinating.

Uncertainty is one of the biggest ongoing problems in business. John H. Patterson of NCR said: "An executive is a man who decides; sometimes he decides right, but always he decides."

> Indecision is debilitating; it feeds upon itself; it is, one might almost say, habit-forming. Not only that, but it is contagious; it transmits itself to others. . . . Business is dependent upon action. It cannot go forward by hesitation. Those in executive positions must fortify themselves with facts and accept responsibility for decisions based upon them. Often greater risk is involved in postponement than in making a wrong decision.
>
> —H. A. Hopf

Once I heard a man tell a story about "Obvious Jones." Obvious Jones became successful by following the motto of always "doing the obvious." When he was plagued with a big problem, he just kept whittling away at the problem by doing the obvious things that he should do until finally the solution fell into place. I used to keep a little sign on my desk that read, "Do The Obvious." The sign is no longer there. I don't need it because I have internalized that motto. I just look for a part of the problem that has an obvious solution. I accomplish the part which in turn makes another part of the problem obvious, etc. This technique is deceptively simple. You will not believe its effectiveness until you try it. I know that it works for me. I recommend it to you.

The other effective tools for combating procrastination are planning and staying well organized. We cover planning, in the section on "Management By Objectives" and staying well-organized in "You've Got To Get Organized."

The most important element of dependability is the opinion of other people that you can be depended upon to do that which you are supposed to do if it is possible and within your power to do so. Further, they can expect your very best efforts, and *very importantly*, that when it becomes obvious to you that you will not complete a task at all, or on time, you will advise the interested parties.

Above everything else, dependability is what I desire in anyone who works with me. You should almost never have to ask people who report to you if they have done what you have asked them to do. You should be able to assume that when you give someone an assignment, unless you hear to the contrary, it will get done.

A young man starting out on a new job can make a profound effect on his manager by saying, "Sir, I may not always accomplish what you ask me to do, but unless I come to you and tell you that I did not do it, you can assume that it was done." If you were this new man's manager, you would know that at least he understands what being dependable is all about and that he had enough confidence to commit himself and lay it right on the line. Any manager should be impressed with such an attitude.

When you are trying to sell yourself to someone else, you can display your track record, you can say all of the good words, show an impressive financial statement or what have you, but in the final analysis what people are really buying is you and the degree to which they feel that they can DEPEND on you.

The subjective part of dependability comes into play when a project fails or a projection is not met. If a building is supposed to be complete in six months and the monsoons set in and it rains everyday and it takes nine months, is the builder undependable? Or do we blame God for being undependable? If God is undependable, who is man to think he can be more dependable? It is unrealistic to define a dependable person as one who *always* accomplishes that which he said that he would accomplish. In almost any undertaking there is an inherent risk factor. But you can't use this as a "cop-out." Realism is the key. When you make projections and commitments, they should be based on certain assumptions that take into consideration any risk factors. Any deviation from course should be reported promptly. In this way, you can go a long way toward protecting one of your most important, but often abused, assets—your *dependability*.

■ Let Them Know You Were There

I believe that it was Abraham Lincoln who said that "it is better to remain silent and be thought a fool, than to open your mouth and remove all doubt." With all due respect to Mr. Lincoln, I am sorry that he provided this convenient "cop-out" for failure-avoiders. If you are truly interested in seeking success as opposed to avoiding failure, you had better forget Mr. Lincoln's advice. Whenever I attend a meeting or am in a group, I make it my business to make them remember that I was there. I get involved. I ask questions. It is an old cliche but "you get out of it what you put into it." I would go further than that. I would say that as long as you are giving of yourself, you cannot give as much as you will get back in return.

When you attend a meeting, *get involved*. Otherwise, you will sit there like a sponge, trying to sop up information. The problem with this is that you give no direction to the discussion. You have to go with the tide and listen to whatever the people who are "speaking up" want to talk about.

Learning to speak on your feet is a valuable vehicle to success. You learn to speak on your feet by *speaking on your feet*. I have never taken a course in public speaking or affiliated with any group whose purpose it was to teach people to be better public speakers. I think perhaps I could have speeded up the learning process if I had. The point is that the training helps; but if you want to learn to speak on your feet, you can by doing two things; decide that you want to, and then do it.

The first few times I spoke on my feet I was petrified. I felt weak. My skin was clammy. I clutched my notes like a drowning man with a straw. Since then, I have given many, many talks to various types of groups without any nervousness. I look forward to it because the more of it I do the better I get. Perhaps I am not a polished public speaker, but I do manage to say what it is that I want to say. I seldom depend on notes, and I prefer to speak in a conversational style as I would speak to you if I were sitting across the desk from you. I try to speak in a style that I find appealing when I listen to others speak. There is no right or wrong way as long as you can develop a style that is effective and with which you can be comfortable. The only possible danger in having formal training in public speaking is that at times the people who have had the training come through sounding a little mechanical and do not establish a natural relationship with the audience.

Very possibly the biggest advantage of learning to speak on your feet is that it is the best training for speaking when you are NOT on your feet. It helps you to develop the habit of crystallizing your thoughts in an orderly, concise manner and then presenting them. Public speaking is wonderful training for this. And it will build your ability to sell your ideas to others through improved clarity.

Speech is the most important way that we communicate with one another and the most important way that we are judged by our fellow man. Whenever you hear a man in a high place expressing himself in a substandard manner, you can just bet that he must really excel in another area. Perhaps he is another Einstein or maybe he married the boss's daughter. If you convince yourself that you cannot speak out and express yourself and are not willing to give it the effort, you have saddled yourself with another unnecessary handicap on the road to success.

■ Don't Pay Rent on a Beard

Most of the people with whom you come in contact, even on a regular basis, literally see only about five per cent of you. The rest is covered up with clothes. They see only your head and your hands and it is on this they judge your appearance.

Therefore, why pay rent on a beard, excessively long hair, dirty fingernails or no fingernails at all? If you have a beard, it could cost you a great deal of money every month. For example, if you are a salesman with a beard making $12,000 per year, but could be making another $3000 from people who will not buy from you because you have a beard, you are literally paying $250 a month rent on that beard. Better you should shave it off and wear a false beard when you are away from work.

The same would be true for people who bite their fingernails. Awhile back I noticed that one of our salesmen had the habit of biting his fingernails. I told him that he was lucky he did not have to sell me anything for a living. When he asked why, I told him that I did not make a practice of buying from anyone who bites his fingernails and that if I had conducted his job interview before he came with the company, I never would have hired him until he let his fingernails grow out.

Whether my attitude makes me eccentric or whether I am right or wrong is not important. The fact remains that my attitude toward long hair, fingernails, etc. is not unique. There are many people who share my attitude, so why disqualify yourself with this group? There are many other ways to display your nonconformity and independence without growing a beard.

There are other personal habits and traits that create negative impressions in the minds of those with whom you deal.

The consistent use of poor English is inexcusable. Not being able to speak properly can be a very limiting factor in your success. If you use poor English, it says to the person to whom you are talking that you either do not have the perseverance, the will power, or the sense to overcome this major handicap that requires so little to correct. As the educational level of people continues to increase, using poor English will emphasize more than ever to other people that you "ain't got no smart."

The easiest way to overcome this handicap in a hurry is to ask the members of your family, your close friends or your business associates to help you by correcting you whenever they hear you make a grammatical error. You will probably find that you do not make a lot of different mistakes in your speech, but rather that you consistently make the same mistakes over and over (like using plural subjects with singular verbs). With very little correction and effort, you will find that speaking properly will become a habit.

In summary, if I still have not convinced you, I will close with two questions:

1. "Is there anyone who would *not* do business with you because you *do not have* a beard?"

2. "Is there anyone who would *not* do business with you because you *have* a beard?"

The defense rests.

Poise is a big factor in a man's success. If I were a young man just starting out, I would talk things over with myself as a friend. I would set out to develop poise—for it can be developed. A man should learn to stand, what to do with his hands, what to do with his feet, look his man straight in the eye, dress well and look well and know he looks well. By dressing well I don't mean expensively, but neatly and in taste.

—F. Edson White

■ Play Fair

Is it the truth?
Is it fair to all concerned?
Will it build good will and better friendship?
Will it be beneficial to all concerned?

—Rotary four-way test

While growing up, we were constantly admonished to "do good," live by the Golden Rule, always play fair, etc. You may have gotten the idea that the main reason for "playing fair" was that the master scorekeeper in the sky was constantly watching over you and would give you a black mark any time that you deviated from the straight and narrow.

After we get into business we begin to realize the full extent of the very practical reasons (aside from any moral considerations) for playing fair.

What do we mean by playing fair? The Golden Rule says it all: "Treat all of the people with whom you have dealings in the same manner that you would want to be treated by them." J. C. Penney was famous for building his organization around the "Golden Rule" principle. Christianity embraced the Golden Rule which had been part of religions for centuries before Christ.

The practicality of the Golden Rule is that no man is an island and we are all interdependent. For every action there is a reaction. I can expect to be treated by you as I have treated you. If you "wrong" me, I will not "turn the other cheek," as the Bible suggests that I do. Instead I will follow the principle of "an eye for an eye, and a tooth (maybe even two teeth) for a tooth."

If I am not fair to you, not only can I expect similar treatment from you, but I can also expect side effects which can be even more damaging. I may wrong you in a small way, but you in turn may cause me great difficulty by giving me a bad reputation.

Fortunately, the converse is also true. If I am fair to others in small ways, the value is greatly magnified by the positive effect that it can have on my reputation. Small incidents, both fair and unfair, can have large effects on other unrelated incidents. Some of my biggest sales were made as a result of having previously dealt with people fairly in small, seemingly unrelated matters. You *never* can know at the time the full future impact of fairness. So why take a chance?

> Small kindnesses, small courtesies, small considerations, habitually practiced in our social intercourse, give a greater charm to the character than the display of great talent and accomplishments.
> —Kelty

Playing fair also involves giving your job your very best. Any time that you are not satisfied with your present job, it is your privilege to leave the organization and find something else to do. As long as you stay on the job you are committed to do your best. This extends through the last day that you stay with an organization.

Some people even go beyond this point. After Roger Hallock was officially off the IBM payroll, he returned to make some customer calls with IBM people to insure a smooth transition to the new IBM customer representative. IBM had been fair to him; he felt an obligation to be as fair as he could be to IBM.

In addition to the Golden Rule, playing fair involves integrity, honesty and loyalty.

In business many people seem to play fair in every respect except when it comes to being loyal. Most people want to play fair. When they are disloyal it is because they don't fully understood what fairness means.

You *owe* your loyalty to any group of which you are a part—including the human race. This may be an extreme example, but if you see a man put a suitcase with a bomb in it on an airplane, you owe it to your fellow man to do something about it besides deciding to take the next plane. In a documentary on television, one automobile assembly line worker said that sometimes the steering wheels of cars coming off the assembly line had come off in his hand but that he did not report it "because it was not his responsibility to do so." It IS his responsibility as a member of the organization with whom he works.

You cannot put loyalty in a box on the organization chart. Loyalty to an organization has no boundary lines. It transcends the limits of authority and responsibility as defined in a job description. When you work with an organization, you accept money not only for the work which you do, but also for your loyalty to the whole group. If you are a ribbon clerk, why should you be less loyal to the organization than the president of the company? When *any* worker is not being loyal to the organization, he is to some degree jeopardizing the welfare of all of his fellow workers.

We usually find the lowest degree of group loyalty among those who have the most to lose by not being loyal. If the organization gets into trouble, the people at the lowest levels (who often are the least loyal) are usually the first to be laid off. The most loyal guy in the organization is probably the president, and he will probably be the last to go if the organization gets into difficulty.

Why is management viewed as the "enemy" in many organizations? An organization usually makes it or does not make it as a function of the effectiveness of the management of the organization. Yet it is difficult for management to obtain loyalty from the people at the lower levels. Many people insist that they will be loyal to the management and to the organization ONLY after they have first been loyal to those at their own level.

Here's an example. Two key punch operators work side by side. One does good work, the other "goofs off" and does substandard work. What are the chances that the operator doing good work will attempt to get the poor operator to do better work? If this does not happen, will she "blow the whistle" on the poor operator? No. Nevertheless, the "good" operator *owes* it to the group to take whatever steps are necessary to make sure that the poor operator improves.

Do you disagree? Let's try a test.

Let's take these two operators sitting side by side at key punch machines and place them side by side in a rocket going to the moon. If they *both* do not do an effective job, instead of getting to the moon, they will miss their target—instead of landing on the moon will be doomed to continue on into outer space until they die. Now the test: If you were one of these people, what would be your attitude? Do you still think that you should *not* concern yourself with what the other people in your group are doing?

If you say that you still disagree and that the example of going to the moon is "different," you are really saying that:

1. You should only concern yourself with others in your group when their actions have "life or death" consequences for you personally.
2. What you are doing is not that important.

If either of the above statements reflects your attitude toward your work, Heaven help you. You not only need this book, but also a lot of other help.

Conrad Hilton tells how fortunate he was to have learned the great lesson of playing fair while still a student in military school:

A gentleman told the truth. To lie was a disgrace! To the cadets at Roswell there were no degrees about this. You either spoke the truth— or you didn't.

If, in the course of my own life, I have lost some small things by carrying my regard for truth to an excess. . . . I can only believe I have gained greater things by it than I have ever lost. . . . I personally have been able to do business with some pretty rough characters; but I have never been able to deal with a liar.

In general, the more successful people are, the more ethical they are. This is for a very good reason. When a person is in the process of satisfying the lower levels of his basic animal needs there is often a tendency to put less emphasis on ethical behavior. The "law of the jungle" prevails. As a person becomes more successful, however, success brings a sense of self-fulfillment, achievement, and pride and accomplishment. Any infraction of the rules, no matter how insignificant, becomes magnified in his own mind as he progresses up the ladder.

To thine own self be true, and it must follow as the night the day, thou canst not then be false to any man.

—William Shakespeare

Problems and Crises

One day as Chicken Little was walking through the woods, an acorn fell on her head. "Dear me" she thought, "the sky is falling." I must go and tell the king.

WE ARE ALL somewhat like "Chicken Little." Things are going along pretty well when all of a sudden an acorn hits us on the head (we have a little trouble) and we think the sky is falling in. We begin to get a bit panicky, and as a result we begin to lose some of our effectiveness. Events that under normal conditions we would take in stride, now suddenly begin to appear as problems. Actually, there can be a "domino effect" with problems. One problem creates another, which in turn creates another, etc. When this happens, we have the momentum going against us and it might appear that the sky IS falling in.

If you assume that you are having a streak of bad luck, you run the risk of assuming a defeatist attitude and just HOPING

167

that your luck will change. Unfortunately, this usually will not "hack it."

In watching professional basketball games on television, it is interesting to watch the momentum swing back and forth from one team to the other. Watch for it yourself sometime. When the momentum obviously is going against one of the teams, that team will call "time out." Calling time out hopefully kills the negative momentum and also gives the team an opportunity to huddle with the coach and decide what tactics they will use to regain positive momentum.

This is exactly what we should often do in business, At times, the momentum *is* going against us, and when it does we should in essence call time out. It is not as simple in business as it is in basketball, because there are no real time outs in the game of business. However, we can stop and regroup, analyze our problems, and determine what it is that we can do to arrest the negative momentum and start "digging out." Normally we do just the opposite. When we have negative momentum going against us, instead of calling time out and studying our problem, we step up the activity. We frantically start working harder doing the same things we have been doing all along. It is a little like being in quicksand. When you start sinking, this is not the time for more frantic activity. It is the time to remain calm and rational and to minimize your activity as you carefully begin to extract yourself from the quicksand.

Amazingly, people in trouble sometimes say they are too busy fighting the problem to stop and plan how they are going to get out of trouble. They say they do not have time to plan. The truth is that they do not have time NOT to plan.

> The ability to keep a cool head in an emergency, maintain poise in the midst of excitement, and to refuse to be stampeded are true marks of leadership.
>
> —R. Shannon

It often happens that right after a woman has a baby she will experience what is known as the "baby blues." In the same way, people get promoted and right afterwards experience the "baby blues" about their new jobs. As soon as they are promoted they suddenly seem to have more problems than ever before.

They are right. They do have more problems, although I prefer to call them challenges. As a person moves up through the ranks he should recognize that he will be confronted with more challenges, problems, or whatever you want to call them. If you do not realize that this is what people at higher and higher levels do, you are surely headed for trouble if you aspire to progress in your organization. It stands to reason that the lower the level, the more routine the work, and the higher the level, the more problems and challenges. Most of the "bitching" in an organization is done by those at the lowest level in spite of the fact that they have the fewest problems. The higher the level, the more the problems and the more the need for a positive attitude. Bitching at the higher levels is a luxury that a manager cannot afford.

I am president of an organization with about one hundred and twenty employees. One of my prime responsibilities is to maintain a positive attitude about the business in spite of the fact that I spend most of my time dealing with what most people would consider problems. Many of the things I work on that other people might regard as problems, I look on as being rather routine. I am used to it. I am experienced in dealing with these matters. It is what keeps the game interesting. Problems are also relative. I am sure that the president of the United States handles many matters rather routinely that would take on major significance if they were my responsibility. He is used to it. I am not.

The man who is bigger than his job keeps cool. Confident that he is equal to any emergency, he does not lose his head. He refuses to become rattled, to fly off in a temper, to stamp and holler and swear. The man who would control others must be able to control himself.

—B. C. Forbes

■ If at First You Don't Succeed, Perhaps You Should Quit

We have all been admonished that "If at first we don't succeed, we should try, try again." Try again until what happens? Perhaps until we are wiped out . . . I am a great believer in what Vince Lombardi, the football coach, called "second effort." However, I disagree with the old adage, try, try again unless it means "If at first you don't succeed, try, try again until you reach the predetermined point at which you admit that you are wrong—and quit."

The commodity market can teach you a lot of lessons about when to quit, although the price of the lessons leaves a lot to be desired. It is a favorite saying in the stock market and in the commodity market that you should "cut your losses and let your profits run." What they don't tell you is at what point to cut your losses and how far to let your profits "run."

"Cut your losses and let your profits run" doesn't mean a great deal. When I had $50,000 in my commodity account, people would ask, "Why don't you get out?" 'I replied that I was letting my profit run and thought that the price of wheat would go higher. When I had $75,000, I thought that wheat would go higher, as I did when my account stood at $93,000. At this point, wheat was selling for about $1.60 per bushel and many people who were holding wheat, including yours truly, thought that wheat would go to $2.50 per bushel. When the price of wheat first started to go down, I determined that it was only a fluctuation and that it would shortly resume its upward move. In retrospect, it is clearly obvious that I should have gotten out when I was ahead.

PREDETERMINE what you will do under various circumstances. In the heat of battle, it is very difficult to make rational decisions. The commodity market moves so fast that a slight delay in making a decision can be very costly. Ever since that experience I have always attempted to make a risk assessment ahead of time when I could maintain my objectivity and think through a situation on a very rational basis. You should decide at what point you will give up a losing endeavor. Also determine, as best you can, what the possible extenuating circumstances would be that would cause you to reassess your decision to give up on a project. For example, you may have decided to quit a job if you had not gotten a promotion by June 30. On June 15 it is announced that a new vice-president will be named on July 31. You are being considered for the position. Obviously, you should reassess your earlier decision to quit if you did not get a promotion by June 30.

Failure to make a decision can be very costly. But, in fact, failure to make a decision is, in effect, *making* a decision. You have decided NOT TO ACT. Unfortunately, too many people do not realize that not making a decision is of significance until it is too late. The decision is made by default as a result of your indecision.

The commodity market and the stock market also disprove the old adage that you have to be right only fifty-one per cent of the time in order to be successful. The percentage of the time that you are right or wrong does not mean anything unless you give weight to the importance of each decision. In the commodity market for example, you can be wrong many, many times and take small losses; but be right on relatively few important decisions and you can be very successful. The converse is also true. In business, you can be right ninety-nine per cent of the time, but if you are wrong one per cent of the time on decisions that could bankrupt you, your excellent batting average does not mean much. In fact, it doesn't mean anything. Don't delude yourself into thinking that it is important how often you are right or wrong. What *is* important is the *matters* about which you are right or wrong.

One reason it is so hard for most of us to admit that we are wrong and quit is "ego." We find this not only in our individual lives but in business. Businessmen often will go far beyond the point at which they should have given up.

Peter Drucker refers to this as "managerial ego." As you read the following quote from his book, "Managing for Results," think not only in terms of managerial ego in business but also of the times that you, as an individual in your private life, fall victim to the same tendency:

> This is the product that should be a success—but is not. But Management has invested so much in the product by way of pride and skill that it refuses to face reality. The product, management is convinced, will succeed tomorrow—but tomorrow never comes. And the longer the product fails to live up to expectations, the more does management become addicted to it, and the more key resources are pumped into it.

The next time that you are contemplating "try, try again," reconsider in light of the managerial ego. Maybe instead of trying again you should "hang it up."

■ When They Beat on Your Cage

Most of us lived in neighborhoods where there were always a few "bullies" who enjoyed kicking you around for recreation. You will still find bullies in the business world. They have gotten bigger, older and uglier. Now they wear coats and ties. But they act the same.

You still must deal with these people in the same way that you used to. If you let them start "beating on your cage" and get by with it, they will never let up. I believe in going to great lengths to avoid unpleasant confrontations in business, but when people start confusing *not* fighting with *not being able* to fight, it is necessary that you get them straightened out.

Because of the competitive nature of business and the aggressive nature of many people in business, there is a tendency for some individuals to "push you" as far as they can just as a matter of course. This is the way they deal with everyone. Those who can be pushed, they push. This type of person normally will respect you for letting him know *you* are not going to be pushed around.

A man can be an excellent manager—aggressive, competitive and highly persuasive. But if he unconsciously intimidates his people or tends to push them around at times, this kind of manager will build a staff of "yes men."

Don't let your people become "yes men." Your employees should be encouraged to tell you that "you are crazy as hell" if they feel so inclined. Such a comment is highly *complimentary* to a *strong* manager for it indicates that he has established good communication with his people. (This is based on the assumption that such a comment represents honest disagreement and not disrespect for the manager.) It is a cardinal sin for a manager to ever take disciplinary action against one of his people for honest disagreement, no matter how strongly he chooses to express himself. The first time a manager does this, he cuts his lines of communication with his people.

If I were being interviewed tomorrow for a position with a company, I would ask the man to whom I would report if I would be able to feel free in telling him when I think he is wrong and to tell him "to get off my back" when he leans on me unduly hard. If I did not get a satisfactory answer I would not go with that organization. I would also check with some of the other people in the organization who report to this man to get their comments on this subject.

You may think I am giving you an easy lesson in how to get fired. You are better off being fired than you are working for an organization in which you can get fired for expressing yourself and being a man. I have raised a lot of hell at times with people in our organization and at times they have given it back to me with equal force, but in spite of disagreements and arguments at times, I have *never* been guilty of terminating a man for disagreeing with me or "bucking up" to me whenever he felt that I had "wronged him" and was beating on his cage.

■ Beware the Dog!—the Underdog

Damon Runyon said "The race is not always to the swift, nor the battle to the strong—but that's the way to bet."

This is somewhat contrary to our American way of life. This country was started by "underdogs" and this is a part of our heritage. As a result, I feel rather unpatriotic in suggesting that I am all for cheering for the underdog but when it comes to betting I agree with Runyon.

There are underdogs and there are underdogs. We all go through periods when we are temporarily underdogs. But then there are chronic underdogs who never seem to be able to catch up with their peer groups and are always "an hour late and a dollar short." And yet some of these people are the most smooth talking people you will ever encounter. Words are their only weapons, and they have an excuse for every setback they ever experienced.

It is fine to cast your lot with the "Davids" who, you *believe*, can cope effectively with the "Goliaths" and cut them down to size. After all, big companies started off as little companies. The key is to *believe* in the concept and in the people with whom you work. If you do not do this and pursue a course based on "hope," you are betting against the house. And, when you bet against the house, sooner or later they grind you out.

Perhaps you've heard the story of the fellow who was walking down the road when a beautiful nude girl ran past him, followed closely by a man in a white suit chasing after her. Then he saw another man in a white suit running many yards behind, huffing and puffing, with a bucket of sand in each hand. The startled gentleman stopped the second man in the white suit and asked what was going on. The man in the white suit replied that the beautiful girl was an inmate of the mental institution and everyday she pulled off all of her clothes and escaped. The gentleman said that was fine, but why the buckets of sand. The man in the white suit replied, "I caught her yesterday and this is my handicap."

Bet on whom you want; I'm betting on the guy without all the sand.

It has taken me many years to develop to some extent an intuitive feeling whenever I am dealing with a chronic underdog. Without knowing exactly why, I get an intuitive feeling that I will regret the day if I ever do business with this person. The times I have gone against my intuitive feelings, I have gotten "clobbered."

Emerson once said "What you are thunders so loudly that I cannot hear what you are saying." Look beyond the words to the actions and the concepts. You are judged not on the basis of what you say, but on what you do.

■ How You Can "Sell" Me

We are all salesmen everyday of our lives. We are selling our ideas, our plans, our enthusiasms to those with whom we come in contact.
—Charles M. Schwab

This will be the most immodest statement that I will make in this book. *I am a very good salesman.* Immodest, but true. My record as a salesman speaks for itself.

We are all salesmen. In dealing with other people we are continually called on to sell ourselves or our ideas. You sell people to get them to do what you want them to do. You have to sell to your children, your wife, your business associates (whether they be under you, over you or next to you). You sell customers, creditors, etc. We are all in the business of selling.

The comments in this chapter have to do specifically with those who are called salesmen, although much of the material is applicable to any of the other selling situations in which we all are involved.

Selling is another of the great paradoxes in business. It is so simple and yet so difficult. It is simple because there are so few fundamentals involved, and yet it is difficult because the fundamentals are so frequently ignored.

I will admit that there are different ways that successful salesmen sell. Therefore, I cannot tell you *exactly* how *you* should sell. However, I can tell you *exactly* how *I can be sold*. I have been in hundreds of situations where I was a salesman and I know from this experience that I am not too different from the typical buyer.

The following points are not ranked in order of importance, but rather in logical sequence from the initial contact to the final sale:

1. *Don't telephone my office and leave word for me to call you.*

The only exception to this would be if I already know you well enough for you to take this liberty, or if your position earns you the right to do so. (If you are president of the United States, the Pope or Howard Hughes, I will understand.) You are trying to sell me. If I had wanted what you are trying to sell, I would have telephoned you to begin with.

2. *Telephone me the morning of the day that you want to see me.*

If I tell you that I cannot see you today, then you should logically ask when you could see me. If you call and ask for an appointment two weeks from now, this says to me one of two things. Either you are trying to "trap" me by asking for an appointment way off in the future, or you are saying that you are so damn busy that you cannot work me into your schedule for two weeks. This tells me that you want to talk to me at your convenience and not at mine.

3. *Come by without an appointment if you wish.*

I will talk to you if I am not involved with something that cannot be set aside temporarily. I do not recommend this approach for the following reasons:

    a. I may be out of the office or not be able to see you, which results in a waste of your time.

    b. By telephoning me first, you can make sure I am a valid prospect before investing your time in making a personal call on me.

    c. If you telephone me first it tells me that not only do you respect my time, but that you also respect your own time.

If you do choose to come by without an appointment, you sure as hell better not tell me that you "just happened to be in the neighborhood." I do not care to be an "afterthought." If you were in the neighborhood, I want to think that it is because I am important enough for you to come here to see ME, not someone else.

4. *Bring fingernails.*

If you bite your fingernails, you had better wear gloves. Otherwise I will not buy from you. If you must wear a beard, I will try very hard to listen to what it is that you have to say in spite of my preoccupation with the growth on your face. I also prefer that you not wear white socks and black shoes unless you are anxious for me to know that you are from somewhere out in the "sticks."

5.   *Don't bring "Charlie McCarthy" with you.*

For the benefit of you younger people, Charlie McCarthy was a famous ventriloquist's "dummy" of the nineteen thirties and forties. If you are going to bring someone into my office with you, I want them to make noise. After a man has been in my office for awhile without saying anything, I find myself looking for the string coming out of the back of his neck. (My ex-partner, Roger Hallock, took a sales trainee with him into a prospect's office one time while Roger was still with IBM, and the trainee went to sleep sitting in the chair in front of the prospect. I suspect that some of the "dummies" who have been in my office have learned to sleep with their eyes open.)

6.   *Leave your suitcase at the office.*

It frightens me when a salesman comes in with a huge suitcase full of material. He may be like "the man who came to dinner" and stayed for months. The less you can bring into my office, the better. There is a direct relationship between how much a salesman knows and the size of the case he brings into your office. The more he knows, the smaller the case. The less he knows, the larger the case.

7.   *Don't smoke without asking.*

Even if I am smoking, it is a common courtesy to ask me if you may smoke. If I am not smoking, it is even more important that you ask. I may violently object to cigarette smoke.

8.   *If you must cuss, let me cuss first.*

I have been known to use a "salty" word or two at times, but I object to someone doing the same in my office until I have first done so. Along the same line, please don't tell me any jokes. I am already dealing with too many comedians.

9.   *Don't bring your "I Am a Salesman" sign.*

Some guys come waltzing into my office with "I Am a Salesman" written all over them. They could not be more obvious if they had a sign to that effect hanging around their neck. Don't "sell me." *Help me to buy.* Don't "pitch" like a circus barker. Talk to me as you would to your own brother. Keep it loose. Don't make me feel uneasy because you are feeling uneasy. Soften me up first. Comment on my roll-top desk, a picture on the wall, anything to "break the ice." Here are some hints for helping you forget that you are here to sell me something:

a. Don't "butter me up" with false flattery.

b. Be pleasant but don't paste a grin on your face that makes you look like "a mule eating briars." Smile the way you would smile at a good friend sitting with you in a fishing boat.

c. *Leave off the superlatives.* Don't tell me that your product is "fantastic" (a greatly over used word which means "exceedingly or unbelievably great"), or that your product is "unbelievable." If I can believe that man has been to the moon, why would I have trouble believing your product? Besides, why would I want to buy something that cannot be believed?

d. *Don't "name drop."* I don't really give a damn who you know so don't try to impress me with names. However, I would be very interested in the names of the people who use your product or service.

e. *Don't call me "mister."* I prefer to be called by my first name. This can be a little delicate. At times, you can sense when you should call someone by his first name, but you should always ask first if it is all right if you do so. Often a prospect will tell you to call him by his first name. I strive to get on a first-name basis as soon as possible. It establishes a relationship on a friendly basis more so than by calling each other "mister."

f. *Don't try to "sell me" with your personality.* Your personality is very important and with it you can persuade me to pay attention and sell me a desire to buy from you if I can justify it. The real test of whether or not I buy from you will be the degree of product knowledge that you have.

g. *Don't sit across the desk from me.* This may seem like a minor point, but I purposely have my office arranged in order that there are no physical barriers between me and the people who come in. A desk between me and a prospect has always been a "hang-up" of mine. When I am in a prospect's office, I always position myself, if possible, so that there is no desk or other physical barrier between us. Physical barriers can lead to mental barriers.

h. *Throw out the sales manual.* Don't keep asking any questions, the obvious purpose of which is just to get me to start answering yes. Don't use any other gimmicks that I have been reading in books on salesmanship for twenty years. When you are calling on an old salesman, you had better low-key your approach. This gets back to knowing your prospect. The more "savvy" the prospect, the more low-key should be your approach.

10. *Do not display any lack of confidence or belief.*

If you lack confidence or belief in yourself or in your product, it will show. If you are not confident, how can I be expected to have confidence in you and in your product? Don't let me intimidate you. You must make up your mind before you come into my office that IF I need your product, you are going to help me buy it. It is true that the sale begins in the mind of the salesman. Notice that I said "IF I need your product." I strongly object to a salesman coming into my office with the attitude that I am going to buy, whether I need it or not. It is good sales psychology to let the prospect know early in the game that you are not sure he needs your product, and that is what you are to determine by being there. This immediately helps to get the prospect off the defensive. He is saying to himself "Hell, this guy is on my side." Paul G. Hoffman said that "Salesmanship consists of transferring conviction by a seller to a buyer."

11. *Let me help you sell me.*

Early in our discussion, ask me what it will take to sell me. Ask me what I am after. Don't sit there and try to sell me on price when I am interested in fast delivery. Ask me about my problems, then "shut up and listen." Salesmen are natural born talkers and it takes discipline to learn to listen. Respond to what

I am interested in. If I want to know what time it is, don't tell me how the watch works. Talk in terms of results and put me in the picture. I am interested in what you can do for me and I may have very little interest in your telling me the history of your company.

12. *Take notes and ask questions.*

Salesmen irritate me when they don't take notes of important points, when they don't ask a single question after a rather lengthy discussion. I have often asked a salesman who is guilty of doing these things if he is a memory expert or a genius. When he tells me that he is neither, I tell him I assumed he was because he did not take notes. This seemed to indicate that he could either remember everything I said or he did not think I had said a damn thing worth noting. As for his failure to ask questions, I might tell him that I didn't know of any other geniuses who were in sales besides me, but *he* must be because he understood everything I told him without question.

One of the best ways to sell someone is to sell him by not understanding. Even if you do understand everything that was said, ask at least one question. This says to your prospect "I understand everything that you have told me except for this one point." When I am selling, I always ask *at least* one question. It is not a sign of weakness to ask a question, it is a sign of a weakness not to ask questions. If you don't ask me questions, I will assume that you are stupid. I'll probably be right.

13. *Don't try to "snow" me.*

Give me the facts, not a lot of "crap" in an attempt to confuse the issue. If you don't know the answer to a question I ask, tell me that you don't know but that you will find out. Speak English. Don't lay a lot of words on me that are peculiar to your type of business with which I am not familiar. And don't refer to your machines with a lot of different model numbers that mean nothing to me. I am interested in what they will do and how much it will cost.

14. *NO, is not a pause in the conversation.*

Some salesmen will tell you that with them no is just a pause in the conversation. It had better be more than that when you are calling on me. When I say no or raise an objection, I expect you to respond in some way rather than to ignore it. If I raise an objection and you know that it will be covered later in the presentation, ask if it is all right if we defer answering that objection until we get to that specific point. (Don't make the mistake of not getting back to my objection later.) When I say no to buying your product, don't ignore it but instead walk softly until you can "open my mind" again. Otherwise you will appear to be coming on too strong.

15. *I am not buying a Mexican blanket.*

Don't "horse trade" any more than you have to. I know that you need a little room for negotiating the price, but don't make it like haggling over the price of a blanket down in Mexico. If you cut the price every time that I say no to your proposition, how can I ever know when I have gotten your very best price? If you have to cut the price, try to do it by cutting out something that you are willing to give me in return. For example, you might have a situation where you would have to give me two-week delivery instead of one-week delivery if you cut the price. Even if you are a "price cutter" try to make it sound like you aren't. Being an old salesman myself, I don't like to buy from price cutters.

16. *Don't knock the competition.*

It is all right to draw favorable comparisons between your product and that of the competition, but be careful not to "blast" your competitor. I also prefer that you do not act as if you have a monopoly. If you are rather sure that the subject of your competition is going to come up anyway, bring up the subject before I do. This tends to take the bullets out of my gun. You can assume that I am wondering about your competition even if I do not bring up the subject. It is better to get it out on the table in order that you can draw a favorable comparison, rather than have me make the comparison later, perhaps with your competitor. Incidentally, I have also found it effective to bring out the features which your competition claims as advantages. This gives you an opportunity to comment on them, but in a way that puts your product in a favorable light. Later, when your competition is talking to your prospect, the impact of his advantages is softened. The prospect has already heard them once from you, slanted in a way that is favorable to you. The key word here is "judgment." All of this has to be done in good taste and in complete honesty, or it will backfire on you.

17. *Don't create credibility gaps.*

Be dependable. Don't be late for the appointment or I will assume that you will also be late in delivering the merchandise. Do what you tell me that you are going to do. If you tell me that you are going to write me a letter, do it. If you tell me that you will have a proposal to me by next week, have it by next week.

18. *Respect my time.*

After we have concluded our business, "get the hell out" unless I take the initiative to want to "shoot the bull" and talk longer. I also like to be asked in advance how much time I have to spend with you. This way you can pace your presentation accordingly. It also gives me a good excuse to run you out of my office at the end of the allotted time, if I so choose.

19. *Ask for the order.*

It embarrasses me to have to tell a salesman to do this. The whole purpose of selling is to "close," to "get the order." I continue to be shocked at the number of so-called salesman around who have a hard time asking for the order. If you ask me once and I say no, don't give up. Give me more information and then try again. The best sales that I have ever made have been after I had been told no at least once.

If you will follow these guidelines, you will sell more business accidentally than most salesmen do on purpose.

Unless the man who works in an office is able to "sell" himself and his ideas, unless he has the power to convince others of the soundness of his convictions, he can never achieve his goals. He may have the best ideas in the world, he may have plans which would revolutionize entire industries. But unless he can persuade others that his ideas are good, he will never get the chance to put them into effect. Stripped of ıon-essentials, all business activity is a sales battle. And everyone in business must be a salesman.

—Robert E. M. Cowle

Personal Management by Objectives— Getting It Together

Three men were laying brick.
The first was asked: "What are you doing?"
He answered: "Laying some brick."
The second man was asked: "What are you working for?"
He answered: "Five dollars a day."
The third man was asked: "What are you doing?"
He answered: "I am helping to build a great cathedral."
Which man are you?

—Charles M. Schwab

THE ABOVE STORY of the three bricklayers has an unhappy sequel. The bricklayer who was building a great cathedral was fired. He was supposed to be building a post office. The bricklayer had the right idea in that he was motivated by an objective. Unfortunately, his objective was not compatible with the group of which he was a part. We will want to take a closer look at this man, but first let's take a look at the other two bricklayers.

The bricklayer who was "laying some brick" is the easiest to analyze. He is task-oriented, *NOT* objective-motivated. He sees laying brick as an end in itself. He probably does not know what he is building and could not care less. You can assume that his productivity is below average and that he does just enough to get by. He is indifferent to management. He belongs to the union but probably does not go to the meetings. On and off the job he is likely to be pretty dull. There is a good chance that he will die broke. He lives day to day and will wake up some morning to find that he is too old to keep laying brick. You can find his counterpart in the sales field in the character created by Arthur Miller in the play and later the movie, *The Death Of A Salesman*. Willy Loman, had been selling for thirty-four years without any real objectives. He made good money during his earlier years, but as he grew older and slowed down, his sales diminished and he found himself broke at the age of sixty-four. There was no professionalism in his sales approach. Willy felt that "contacts is what you need, that is what counts." His wife described him as "just like a little boat in search of a safe harbor." He liked the game when he was good at it, but never really understood the objective of the game.

As for the bricklayer who was working for five dollars a day (now they make more than that in an hour), we would have to know a lot more about him before we could come to any definite conclusions. This man is money-oriented. We should establish the "need" that this man wants to satisfy with money. If he is satisfying a low level of need—such as the need to feel secure —once he has achieved security he may become task-oriented like the first bricklayer and be less effective on the job. However, if money represents a vehicle for satisfying his need for a feeling of importance or self-fulfillment, he will probably remain highly-motivated. Unfortunately, his observation that he is working for money may indicate that he gets very little satisfaction or enrichment from his job. What really motivates him is found outside of the job environment.

Now let's take a look at the bricklayer whose personal objective was to build a great cathedral—although the objective of the organization was to build a post office. The blame for the firing of the bricklayer probably has to be shared by the organization. Chances are that the organization never got a commitment from the bricklayer that he would agree to build a post office. This is a very significant point. If an organization does not make it clear to its people what the objectives of the organization are, the people in the organization will decide for themselves where they "think" that the organization is going.

Although the organization has a responsibility to let people know what its objectives are, this does not relieve the individual from the responsibility of identifying the objectives of the organization and the part he plays in accomplishing these objectives.

This brings us down to the most effective method for a group or an individual to manage its affairs. The method is commonly known as Management By Objectives.

Management By Objectives includes not only the management of group activities, but also the management of an individual's activities and how his activities relate to the group of which he is a part. Therefore, whether you are an individual specialist, a manager, or someone who aspires to be a manager, Management By Objectives is of value to you.

Management By Objectives can be defined as achieving objectives through *planning*, *organizing* and *controlling* the activities of people.

The first step is obviously the setting of objectives. We will define objectives as the *measurable* things to be done within a given period of *time*. Good objectives have the following characteristics.

1. *Written.* If you cannot define an objective in black and white it is not an objective.
2. *Challenging but realistic.* Objectives must be attainable or they lose their motivational value. They should neither be so high that it is not possible to make them nor so low that it does not represent a challenge.

3. *Specific and definite.* They should be clearly measurable (dollars, units, etc.) and have a time set for their accomplishment.
4. *Ranked as to priority.*
5. *Compatible* with the objectives of other groups or individuals within the organization as well as with the objectives of the total organization.
6. *Measurable.* Progress toward the objective can be reviewed and measured on an interim basis for possible changes in objectives or for taking corrective action.

When good objectives have been established with the desired characteristics, Management By Objectives will enable the group to realize the following advantages. It:

1. results in being able to *plan.*
2. allows more personnel to realize a sense of participation and achievement.
3. promotes effective delegation in that decisions are made at the lowest levels at which they can *properly* be made. It also results in people not being told what to do but rather that for which they are responsible.
4. facilitates management control and coordination as a result of responsibilities being clearly defined.
5. improves management training and development.
6. provides evaluation of management and individual effectiveness and a means of determining equitable compensation.
7. facilitates two-way communications. Clearly defined objectives establish a common denominator for communicating.
8. creates a climate for motivation. People can not be motivated to achieve objectives that they don't know about.
9. enables a person to identify his personal goals with the objectives of the organization. They do *not* have to be the same, only compatible. An individual cannot know where he is going within the organization until he finds out where the organization is going.

We have established the desired characteristics of objectives and the advantages of Management By Objectives. The process for achieving the objectives is rather mechanical in nature. Let's review the *planning* aspect and then the *organizing* and *control* features.

Planning can be defined as "the process of determining where you want to go and how you want to get there."

Some of the questions that you will want to ask yourself as you go through the planning process are:

1. Where are we now?
2. Where will we end up if we follow our present path?
3. Where do we want to go?
4. What do we have to do to get us where we want to go (the achieving of our objectives) and how does it affect our situation as it exists today?
5. When will we achieve our objectives?
6. Who is going to carry out the plans?
7. What will the implementation of our plans require in the way of financial, production, material and human resources?
8. Is the overall plan practical? Can we accomplish it or will we have to modify it?

You probably will not be able to appreciate this statement until after you have gone through the planning process: *BUT* "The Process Is More Important Than The Plan". The mechanics of going through the planning process will give you a grasp of the situation, the value of which will probably exceed the value of the plan itself. The plan is a by-product of the planning process. It is during the process that the real work is done.

The advantages of planning are as follows:

1. Provides positive action. No one plans to fail. People plan to succeed. It promotes a positive attitude.
2. Involves the participation of other members of your group.
3. Promotes understanding as to what is to be done.
4. Promotes good organization and focuses attention on the objectives, counteracting task-oriented activity.

5. Promotes good leadership. People know what it is that they want to accomplish.
6. Creates an atmosphere of professional-type management in the group.
7. Identifies risks and enables you to assess them.
8. Leads to action. Planning "makes something happen," with a positive thrust.

Planning is the first element of Management By Objectives. The second element has to do with organizing our people or ourselves in order to carry out our plans and achieve our objectives. The organization chart is one of the methods used in organizing. However, the organizational chart is, at best, just a picture of where everybody fits within the group. The real tool for organizing is the "job description."

A job description covers the specific functions that are to be carried out by each individual. Note that this is a "job" description, not a "person" description. The job description defines the requirements of the job to be done. However, I disagree with those who state that the job description should be structured without regard to individual personalities. Because of the peculiar talents of the individuals within a group, often the job description should take into consideration the strengths and weaknesses of the people with whom you have to work. This is particularly so in smaller companies.

The overriding considerations in establishing job descriptions have to do with the objectives that you want to achieve. The job description is made up of four elements:

1. *Functions to be performed.* This defines the responsibilities of the job.
2. *Authority to go with the functions.* This defines the limits of authority for the job and should be compatible with the amount of responsibility contained in the job. Obviously, a person should not be responsible for more than he has the authority to control.
3. *Relationship with others.* This defines how the job relates to other jobs in the organization. It defines to whom the person responsible for the job reports and who reports to him.

4. *Standards of performance.* If any of the four elements of the job description has to be chosen as the most important, it would be the standards of performance. Standards of performance define the conditions that will exist when functions are *satisfactorily* performed by an individual.

We have reviewed the elements of the job description. Now let's take a look at the advantages of having job description:

1. creates an understanding between a man and his manager.
2. clarifies what is required on the job.
3. aids in management development. It provides a common denominator for evaluation of the job a man is doing and his future in the business.
4. creates a "back yard" in which a man can exercise initiative. It clearly delineates the bounds of authority for the job. A man may find it necessary to go beyond his authority, but when he does it will be clear and recognizable.
5. makes it easier to exercise self-control and self-analysis.
6. produces stronger discipline within the organization.
7. makes salary review easier in that a man's performance is more easily measured.
8. eliminates conflict between what the manager thinks you are doing and what you are actually doing. (This was the problem with our friend who was building a cathedral.)
9. does not tell people what to do, it focuses on what they are responsible for.

The job description *includes* the "standards of performance." The standards of performance, in turn, have characteristics which should be mentioned:

1. Standards should be agreed on ahead of time, not after the action has taken place.
2. Standards should be expressed in terms that are measurable, such as: quantity, quality, timeliness and cost.
3. "Blanket" or vague characteristics should be avoided. Some bad examples are: "increase sales," "provide a quality service," "fast delivery." These are subjective and are not clearly measurable.
4. Standards should be challenging but attainable. They should not be impossibly difficult or ridiculously easy.

They should be high enough to make a man extend himself to achieve them.

5. They should be committed to by the man and accepted by his manager.

6. They should be geared to the "key result" areas of the business.

7. The man must understand that anything less than satisfactory performance is not acceptable. The standard is not of excellence but rather a basis on which to measure excellence.

8. They should *not* be kept confidential from other interested parties.

9. The man and his manager should participate in developing the criteria by which he should be measured.

We have now covered the *planning* and *organizational* aspects of Management By Objectives. The third major element is that of *control*. Basically, control can take place *before* the action takes place, *while* the action is taking place, or *after* the action has taken place. Looking at them one at a time:

1. *Pre-operational control*. This is control that is exercised before the action starts. The purpose is to direct the performance toward the objectives that have been predetermined.

2. *Operational control*. This is where the action is, while it is taking place. We can establish check points to see how well we are doing relative to how well we thought we would be doing. For example, we might ask the following questions:

   a. Where are we now?

   b. Where did we say that we would be at this time?

   c. What is the impact of any difference between where we thought we would be at this time and where we actually are?

   d. What are we going to do about the difference between now and the next time that we take a reading?

3. *Post-operational control*. This is control that is exercised after the action has taken place. The preparation of finan-

cial statements at the close of a period would be an example of this type of control. This measures the progress *made* relative to the objectives that we had established. Another type of postoperational control is a performance review. Through performance review, the individual is able to compare how well he did relative to the standards of performance that have been established for his job. We should cover the following in a performance review:

What is this man doing well?

What is the man not doing well?

What help does the man need?

What help will I give him?

What is his potential for promotion?

This is an overview of Management By Objectives. Lengthy books have been written on the subject and at best this chapter will only whet your appetite to learn more about this powerful tool. Think about Management By Objectives not only as a tool for managing others, but as a valuable tool in managing yourself. Perhaps you can encourage the people to whom you report to use this method. I have found Management By Objectives to be of great value to me personally in deciding upon my personal objectives and how I can *plan* to achieve these objectives. It disciplines me to *organize* my resources of time and money and then to exercise self-*control* in measuring where I am, relative to where I planned to be at this time.

If I were to change jobs, before I would accept a position with any organization, I would have to have the answers to the following Management By Objectives questions:

1. Where is this organization now?
2. Where is this organization going?
3. What will be my part (responsibility) in achieving the organizational objectives?
4. What authority will I have in carrying out my responsibilities?
5. How will I be measured, and how will I be compensated?
6. Are you going to tell me what to do, or are you going to tell me what it is that I am responsible for?

If you will give me the answers to the above questions, then I will help you build a post office, not a cathedral.

■ Timing Is All Important

The important point is to be on the spot at the moment most favorable for gaining the desired advantage; and it will be found that of men who get what they want in this world, both those who seem to hasten and those who seem to lounge are always at the right place at the right time.

—David Graham Phillips

Any fundamental that can survive for two thousand years has pretty well proven itself. In the third chapter of Ecclesiastes we are given the basic ground rules for good timing. Ecclesiastes tells us that "For everything its season, and for every activity under heaven its time." These words are as valid today as they were when they were written. In two thousand years, some of the terminology has changed, but the principles remain unchanged. I will quote from Ecclesiastes, and then in parenthesis under each line will give you my version of the modern day terminology for the same thing:

"A time to plant and a time to uproot"

(A time to invest and a time to cash in)

"A time to pull down and a time to build up"

(A time to cut back and a time to expand)

"A time to weep and a time to laugh"

(A time to get serious and a time to keep it loose)

"A time to scatter stones and a time to gather them"

(A time to diversify and a time to concentrate)

"A time to seek and a time to lose"

(A time to look for new opportunities and a time to admit you were wrong)

"A time to keep and a time to throw away"

(A time to tough it out and a time to close down an activity)

"A time to tear and a time to mend"

(A time to shake things up and a time to regroup and start over)

"A time for silence and a time for speech"

(A time to shut up and a time to let 'em know you were there)

"A time for war and a time for peace"

(A time to fight and a time to cool it)

Defining the importance and the characteristics of good timing is easier than telling how to do it. However, good timing is a thread running through this whole book. It is a condition that exists as a result of practicing many of the things that enable you to succeed in spite of yourself. Good timing, like motivation, is woven through all of our activity. It is a contradiction to say that a person seems to do almost everything right but does not succeed because of poor timing. It is another example of cause and effect. The timing is only as good or bad as the cause, which is how well we accomplish other success-producing activity. Many elements of becoming successful are like liquids that can be kept in neat containers. Good timing (and motivation) are like gases that saturate our whole environment.

The greatest enemy of good timing is lack of objectivity. When we act, we do not have the perspective we will have after a period of time has elapsed. When we act we are in the "now" and our objectivity is colored by "time nearness" to the situation. It is only after we get away from our actions in time that we can look back and evaluate them with full objectivity. Today we like the looks of a stock in a particular company, so we buy the stock. Tomorrow we can look back with a little more objectivity and even more after a month or a year. So it is with many of the decisions that we make.

Events in history have to stand the test of time before their real significance can be evaluated. Actions such as President Truman's decision to drop the atom bomb could not be properly evaluated at the time that he made the decision, and even after almost thirty years many people would say that the "jury is still out" on that decision.

It is important that we recognize this lack of objectivity in our timing and make allowances for it. We must mentally detach ourselves as best we can from the "now" and delineate "facts" from "emotions" in making decisions. Human nature leads us to decide what *we want to do*; then we look for the things which will fortify the decision we have *already* made. We fall victim to the "self-fulfilling prophecy." We decide what we want to happen and then we look for all of the reasons why it will happen. We decide to open a tattoo shop. In our enthusiasm for this vehicle to success, we conclude that there is great potential. We tell ourselves that, after all, very few people are tattooed, and even those who are tattooed have plenty of space left for more. There is very little competition. There are no tattoo shops listed in the yellow pages of the phone book. At this point you may be saying that I am being ridiculous. This may be, but I speak with authority. I have done things that are only slightly less ridiculous.

■ There *Is* a Pattern to Success

As it has turned out, I am the big winner in the writing of this book. In the process of crystallizing and summarizing my business philosophy. I have discovered a great "truth." When I began to write, and long after I was well into the project, I would have taken a rather strong position that there is no definable pattern to success. I felt that successful people have become so as a result of a variety of practices which would *not* have established a common denominator for becoming successful. I realize now that I was wrong in my hypothesis. There IS a pattern to success which is found over and over again with amazing consistency in the lives of successful men.

Long before I came to this realization, I had clearly outlined those practices which had worked for me and would, in my mind, make a person successful. It was very gratifying to discover that my personal philosophy for becoming successful was consistent with the pattern that I discovered in writing this book.

To real successful people, almost without exception, success means achieving a sense of self-fulfillment; being able to fulfill one's self as a creative, unique individual according to his own innate potentialities and within the limits of reality.

Most of the people who are really getting the job done in this country, both in government and in business, do not *have* to work for financial considerations. The people who appear to show the least amount of interest in becoming successful are the ones who would have the most to gain financially by doing so.

It is popular to say that successful people are never satisfied. But this implies that they must be "dissatisfied" and perhaps frustrated. We can describe successful people more accurately, as *"unsatisfied."* They have an appetite for more success than they already enjoy, and they *do* enjoy it. Most of the successful people I know thoroughly enjoy their success; and they want more of it.

In order for you to achieve success and become more successful, you must possess the majority of the following characteristics. They represent a summarization of much that has already been covered in this book:

1. Have a strong, positive mental attitude toward yourself, the world in which you live and your ability to become successful. Realize that you are *already* greater than you think you *now* are. You are your own worst enemy, but you can succeed in spite of yourself.

2. Know that success is *within* you, not in the environment. It is portable. You *can* take it with you. If you do not have the vehicle for success in your present situation, either change the conditions or go to another environment.

3. Be aware of the restrictions that have been placed on you, either by yourself or by others. Take the necessary steps to remove as many of these restrictions as possible.

4. Know where you are going. Define your needs and the objectives that will satisfy these needs. This will result in your being motivated. You cannot become motivated to achieve unknown objectives.

5. Believe in yourself and in what you are doing. Your enthusiasm and convictions will be contagious to others, and you will learn to "love the Game."

6. Become educated, formally and informally. Learn from your own experience and the experience of others, both from personal contact and by reading.

7. Concentrate on those things that you do well. However, be constantly aware of your surroundings and have the flexibility of a chameleon should conditions change.

8. Learn what motivates others. Learn to identify their needs. Appeal to these needs in order to create a climate in which other people will do that which you want them to do.

9. Realize that no one needs *money*, and that money is only a potential satisfier of a need. Those who make the most money do so by going after something else. Identify your own needs and seek out those things which will give you a sense of self-fulfillment—the ultimate goal of man. The money will take care of itself.

10. Put in the front end effort. Do more than you are paid to do and later you will be paid for more than you do. Get ahead of the pack and stay there, but always keep glancing over your shoulder to see what the competition is doing. From that source you can learn a great deal.

11. Do not be afraid of challenges that are greater than you have been accustomed to in the past. You can do that which you want to do. Having done so, you will find that you have pulled yourself up further by your own "bootstraps." You will tear down mental barriers which are greater obstacles than physical barriers.

12. Keep it loose. Stay calm and confident. When things are going against you, be particularly rational and objective in your behavior. Stay relaxed in the presence of others. It will win them over to your way of thinking.

13. Look for the reasons why things *can* be done, not why they *cannot* be done. At the same time be realistic. Make a risk assessment as an automatic part of your decision-

making process. Decide the worst that can happen and predetermine a point at which you will abort a given program if it does not live up to your expectations.

14. Spend your time carefully. Put it where it will do the most good. Stay well-organized in order to get the maximum utilization of your time resources.

15. Think big and do big, but remember that doing the big is often a result of doing many little things right.

16. Delegate by telling people what they are responsible for. Don't tell them what to do. You can delegate authority and responsibility, but not accountability.

17. Learn from failure. Recognize that being wrong is an integral part of "making something happen." The more decisions you make the more often you will be wrong. Know when to admit that you were wrong. Otherwise you will fall victim to the "managerial ego" and continue on after you should have quit. Do not "fear" failure, but "respect" it and realize that it is possibly your best vehicle for learning.

18. Just because something *has not* been done does not mean that it *cannot* be done. Seek out advice, but qualify the value of the advice. View situations based on facts not emotions in order that you can maintain your objectivity.

19. Beware the "rapture of the heights." Do not become intoxicated with your success and lose all which you have achieved.

20. When you do tours of duty in Gethsemane, remember that many others have been there before you. View times of worry and stress positively with the knowledge that you will emerge stronger for the lessons you have learned.

21. Don't worry about your job. Concern yourself with the objectives of the group of which you are a part and your job will take care of itself.

22. When you get "fired," don't don sackcloth and ashes. Most successful people were fired somewhere along the line. It is not a disgrace. It is probably just an indication

that your objectives were not compatible with those of the organization. When it is your responsibility to terminate an employee, do not do him the injustice of keeping him on the job because of your own cowardice in failing to face up to *your* responsibility.

23. Find yourself some eagles. Find people from whom you can learn and also eagles on whom you can depend to help make you successful by enabling you to get your work done through their efforts.

24. Be a "loner" at times. Spend time by yourself away from the job environment reflecting on your work. This is probably when you will do your most creative work.

25. You do not have to be a born manager. You can learn to be an effective manager, but before you decide to learn, view yourself objectively. You might be more successful and happier if you do not become a manager.

26. Do not wear your position like a uniform. You can be given the position but you must earn status. When given a new position, do not make waves until you and your people have gotten used to each other.

27. Learn the mechanics of completed staff action and practice on those who report to you, on those to whom you report, and on yourself.

28. Learn the simple mechanics of getting to the heart of the matter by cutting through all of the "crap" and getting down to the bare bones of that which you want to accomplish.

29. Constantly upgrade the quality of the work which you do by constantly eliminating or delegating the least important of your responsibilities.

30. Learn to be an effective communicator. Whenever possible practice two-way communications. Get "feedback" so you can insure that whatever you are communicating is being interpreted in the way that you meant it. Practice Management By Objectives which greatly enhances effective communication.

31. Be dependable. This includes being punctual and being

decisive. Let people depend on you to do that which you are capable of doing and to report to the interested parties promptly whenever you will *not* be able to accomplish a specific objective at all or on time.

32. Results are what count, not the number of hours or the amount of effort expended. Do not let the amount of activity distort the importance of keeping your eye on the results to be achieved. Management By Objectives will enable you to focus on results.

33. Do not use luck as a "cop-out" for not succeeding. Disregard the element of luck, along with any other factor over which you have no real control.

34. If bullies keep "beating on your cage" make sure that they do not misinterpret your *not* fighting for *not being able* to fight. If they push you too far, push back.

35. Do not act impulsively when it is unnecessary. Whenever possible, "sleep on it" in order to develop a little objectivity away from the job environment.

36. Whenever you are a part of any group let them know you are there. Do not hide your light under a bushel. Speak up. Ask questions. In doing so you will participate in providing the leadership of the direction of the group to which you belong.

37. Play fair with all of the people with whom you deal. Deal with people in the same manner that you would have them deal with you. Playing fair includes giving your loyalty to your group.

38. *Always* practice Management By Objectives whenever possible. This is true when you are achieving objectives through other people or through your own efforts.

39. Remember the importance of good timing and the challenge of maintaining your objectivity as you take action. Mentally detach yourself from the "now." Separate facts from emotions in making decisions.

Men are born to succeed—not to fail.

—Henry David Thoreau